GUIDE TO THE RECORDS OF MERSEYSIDE MARITIME MUSEUM

Compiled by
Gordon Read and Michael Stammers

Trustees of the National Museums and Galleries on Merseyside/International Maritime Economic History Association

St. John's, Newfoundland
1995

ISBN -0-9695885-7-7

Contents

Booker Line

Booth Steamship Co. Ltd. (see also Lamport and Holt)

British and African Steam Navigation Co. Ltd.

Britannia Steam Towage Ltd. (see Alexandra Towing
Co. Ltd.)

Thos. and Jno. Brocklebank Ltd. (see also Anchor
Line)

Bulk Cargo Handling Services Ltd. (see Alexandra
Towing Co. Ltd.)

Canadian Pacific Line

Cayzer, Irvine and Co. (see Clan Line)

Charente Steam Ship Co. (see Thos. and Jas. Harrison)

China Mutual Steam Navigation Co. (see Ocean Steam
Ship Co.)

Clan Line

Coast Lines Ltd.

William Cory and Son Ltd.

Cunard Line

Dominion Line

Drysdale Towing Ltd. (see Alexandra Towing Co.
Ltd.)

Elder Dempster and Company

Ellerman Lines

Furness Withy and Co. (see also PSNC)

Glen Line and Shire Line (see also Ocean)

Guinea Gulf Line (see John Holt)

Guion Line

Hall Line (see Ellerman Lines)

Thos. and Jas. Harrison

Alfred Holt (see Ocean Steam Ship Co.)

John Holt and Co. Ltd.

Inman Line

Ismay, Imrie and Co. (see White Star)

Irrawaddy Flotilla Co.

Johnston Warren Ltd.

Kyle Shipping Co. (see Monroe Bros., volume 2)

J.H. Lamey Ltd. (see Alexandra Towing Co. Ltd.)

Lamport and Holt Line (see also Booth Steamship Co.
Ltd.)

Lancashire Shipping Co. Ltd.

Larrinaga and Co.

Leyland Line

Liverpool and Maranham S.S.Co. (see Booth Line)

Liverpool Screw Towing Ltd. (see Alexandra Towing
      Co. Ltd.)
J.J. Mack and Sons Ltd.
Mogul Steamship Co. Ltd. (see volume 2)
J.S. Monks Ltd.
Montreal Ocean Steamship Co. (see Allan Line)
National Line
Nelson Line
North West Tugs Ltd. (see Alexandra Towing Co.
      Ltd.)
Philip Nelson
Ocean Steam Ship Co.
Ocean Transport and Trading plc (see Ocean Steam
      Ship Co.)
Oceanic Steam Navigation Co. (see White Star Line)
Pacific Steam Navigation Co. (see also Furness
      Withy and Co. Ltd.)
Overseas Containers Ltd. (see ACT)
Papayanni Line (see Ellerman Lines)
R. and J.H. Rea (see Elder Dempster)
Royal Mail Steam Packet Co. (see also Pacific Steam
      Navigation Co.)
Sandbach Tinne and Co. (see volume 2)
Shaw Savill and Albion Line
R. Singlehurst and Co. (see Booth Line)
Southampton Steamship Co. Ltd. (Alexandra Towing
      Co. Ltd.)
Straits Steamship Co. Ltd.
Edward W. Turner and Son (see volume 2)
United Molasses Co. Ltd. (see Athel Line)
Warren Line (see Johnston Warren Line)
White Diamond Line (see Johnston Warren Line)
White Star Line
J.H. Worthington (see volume 2)
Yeoward Line
Zillah Shipping Co. Ltd. (see also Coast Lines Ltd.)

ABOUT THE COMPILERS

GORDON READ read Classics at Oxford University before joining the Lancashire Record Office. In 1974 he became the first archivist in the Merseyside County Museums which subsequently became the National Museums & Galleries on Merseyside. He was awarded a Churchill Fellowship in 1985 to pursue his researches on emigration and his currently Secretary of the Association of European Migration Institutions. He has published two books on local history and many articles on emigration and the archives collections of Liverpool.

MICHAEL STAMMERS read History at Bristol University and has worked on the maritime history collections at Liverpool since 1969. He has published a number of books and articles on maritime history including *The Passage Makers*, *History of the Liverpool Black Ball Line* and *Mersey Flats and Flatmen*. He is currently Assistant Editor of the Falkland Islands Journal and serves on the British Commission for Martime History.

Introduction

The Archives of the Merseyside Maritime Museum constitute one of the finest collections of merchant shipping records in the United Kingdom. They include the best run of ship registers, the records of the port of Liverpool – once the second port of the British Empire – local trade associations, shipping companies, merchant houses, port services, charities, shipbuilders, personal and family papers of seafarers plus a wealth of plans, photographs and oral tapes, all linked with an incomparable collection of models, paintings and maritime objects. Every facet of shipping and seaborne trade from the late eighteenth century to the present is covered. While the emphasis is on Liverpool, its ships and seafarers, the coverage is national and international.

The collection dates to 1957 when the shipping department of Liverpool City Museum began a modest Library and Archives with a view to its inclusion in a proposed waterfront maritime museum. In many cases the Archives had a display potential or were part of broader collections of models, pictures and relics. By 1972 the Archives of Brocklebank, Cunard (technical) and the Mersey Docks and Harbour Company's Committee had been received. When the new County Council took over the museums in 1974, an Archivist was appointed who, despite limited resources, was able to secure substantial additions and to order the records according to archival principles. In 1978 Council commissioned a study to assess the feasibility of converting part of the historic but derelict Albert Dock warehouses into a maritime museum, and a pilot project was initiated in 1980. The conversion of the main building at Albert Dock began in 1982 under the auspices of the Merseyside Development Corporation; the archival reading room was opened in 1986 along with the first exhibit galleries. In 1981 the archival premises were approved as a repository under the Public Records Act 1958, which enabled it to hold the Liverpool Register of Merchant Ships – perhaps the single most important collection. The re-organisation or transfer of operations of the major Liverpool-based shipping companies brought further important acquisitions. The gift in 1983 of the collections of Ocean Transport and Trading, which included not only Alfred Holt's original Ocean Steam Ship Co. but also other major shipowners such as Elder Dempster, Cory and Glen and Shire Lines, was especially important. By 1986 the archives of the port authority and of virtually all major shipping companies operating out of Liverpool – Ocean, Brocklebank, Pacific Steam Navigation Co., Lamport & Holt, and Ellerman – were lodged in the museum. The only major exceptions are Booth Line, most of which are presently held by Liverpool City Libraries (although the situation is under review); T. & J. Harrison, which still keeps its own records; and Cunard, whose administrative Archives are held by Liverpool University. The Archives also hold the records of the majority of shipping and a number of import trade associations, as well as of major maritime charities, including the training ships *Conway* and *Indefatigable*.

The year 1986 was also when the Merseyside Maritime Museum attained national status as part of the new National Museums and Galleries on Merseyside, set up by Order-in-Council on 1 April 1986. This led to a revision of Archival collecting policy, which in future was to concentrate on the museum's own records and the maritime archives. The size and strength of the latter justified it, both as a regional and national specialist repository.

In 1981 a typescript summary guide to the Archives department's holdings was produced and was supplemented annually until 1984. This and the work carried out in the early 1980s form the basis of the present *Guide*. The period 1986-1989 was occupied with the transfer of records no longer appropriate and the move of the balance of maritime and NMGM records to the new Maritime Museum and a specially adapted reserve repository. The work of listing continues after the long period of acquisition. This *Guide* reflects work-in-progress and is being published in two volumes. This volume covers the following major collections: records deposited or presented under the Public Records Act, 1958; official organisations including the MDHB, its antecedents and successor; shipping and trade associations; and shipowners.

There are deficiencies in the listings, such as within the MDHB and the John Holt collections; these will be tackled now that the collection has reached the era of consolidation. Work is in progress on a second volume which will be published as soon as possible. This will include sections on: merchants, ships' agents and brokers, stevedoring, warehousing and port services; slavery; emigration; maritime charities and educational establishments; shipbuilding and ancillary industries; maritime family records; individual and personal seafarers' records; solicitors' accumulations; the Bryson collection; special collections, *Titanic* and *Lusitania*; research collections; maps, charts and plans; ships' plans; photographic collections; film and video collections; oral history collections; the Maritime Library (summary of holdings); miscellaneous artificial collections and databases; and non-maritime collections. All these collections are much smaller in bulk than the "big Four" of this volume. It is hoped to publish a comprehensive catalogue of the library at a later date.

This *Guide* should be particularly useful as a supplement and partial replacement for Peter Mathias and Alan Pearsall, *Shipping: A Survey of Historical Records* (Newton Abbot, 1971). This definitive work, still used today, recorded the location of some thirty-five major shipping company Archives, ten of which are affected by entries in this *Guide*. Indeed, in six cases the Archives have passed to the Maritime Archives en bloc. Mathias and Pearsall also omitted references to South American shipping lines included in D.C.M. Platt, *Latin American Business Archives in the United Kingdom* (1965). This is about out of print. In the shipowners' section, several of the individual companies were acquired with collections of historic objects such as ship models. The latter are part of the history of the company concerned and key examples of this type of material are referred to in the individual introductions. This indicates the existence of such material but does not provide comprehensive listings, which are found in the catalogues of the Maritime History department.

Notes on the Access and Use of the Archives

IMPORTANT

Access to the Archives is by the Maritime Archives and Library Reading Room in the Albert Dock Building of the Merseyside Maritime Museum. The current opening times are Tuesdays to Thursdays 10.30 am to 4.30 pm and on other days by prior written appointment. Less-used collections are held at North Street in part of the Central Services Division's premises and are accessible by appointment only. Archives staff can advise on the location of particular records or collections. There is a small charge for a daily or annual reader's ticket. Enquiries in writing are easier to handle given limited staff resources. Complex requests and photographic orders must be in writing and in some cases a charge for staff time may be made. Photographic orders are usually processed by the Museums and Galleries' own staff and can result in long delivery times. Arrangements can be made with approved commercial photographers and the same applies to detailed research work, which can be commissioned from approved researchers via the Archives Department. As the collection becomes better known booking a place in the Reading Room is increasingly advisable.

The Reading Room also offers an extensive collection of books, including runs of major reference sources such as Lloyd's Register and Lloyd's List. Some of these, such as Lloyds List, are on microfilm or fiche. The same applies to some of the Liverpool Ship Registers which are in fragile condition and it is hoped to do the same for the Customs Bills of Entry in the near future. Photocopying is also available but large or delicate volumes and fragile records cannot be copied on conservation grounds. There are also two Archives teaching packs of facsimile documents, *The Leaving of Liverpool* (on emigration) and *Ships and Seafarers in 19th Century*, along with a selection of specialist publications which supplement the stock in the museum's shop. Information on forthcoming seminars, lectures and university courses is also displayed.

This *Guide* is the first point of entry to the Maritime Archives but it must be understood that it provides a summary and not a detailed list of each record within a particular collection. Detailed listings are to be found in the various finding aids, lists and indices in the reading room. Each entry in this *Guide* provides a very brief historical introduction, followed by a listing of the main items, its archival code, its date span and the quantity of records. This is completed by a reference to one or two key printed sources held in the Reading Room. In many cases, these sources may well answer general questions about the history of a particular dock, ship or topic without recourse to the original Archives. In addition, there is a collection of boxes of information on particular subjects which will help the researcher in the initial stages of investigation.

There are also guides to other relevant collections including the National Maritime Museum (volume 2, business records), the Public Record Office, (current guide also in microfiche), Lancashire, Chester, Cheshire and Clwyd Record Offices, as well as guides to a number of overseas repositories.

Finally a note of caution: much has been published on the history of the port of Liverpool and its shipping companies over the years. Using archival material is slow and laborious compared with using printed works, and we recommend that you always ensure that the information you want cannot be found in books. For highly detailed studies, the existing literature can provide a quick way to fill in the background, as well as useful guidance as to what to expect to find in the Archives. If travelling from a distance, it is helpful to do background reading before visiting the museum. This will save time and focus attention on key problems which can only be answered by the material here.

The following books provide an introduction to the port of Liverpool, its ships, docks and seafarers and should be widely available in libraries outside Liverpool. In addition, there is a substantial bibliography at the end of chapter 2 on the history of the port.

Brouwer, N.J. *International Register of Historic Ships*. Oswestry, 1993.

Bryon, R.V. and Bryon, T.H. (eds.). *Maritime Information: A Guide to Libraries and Sources of Information in the United Kingdom*, London, 1993.

Chandler, G. *Liverpool Shipping, A Short History*. London, 1960.

Gardiner, R. (gen. ed.). *Conway's History of the Ship*. London, 1993-1995.

Hope, R. *A New History of British Shipping*. London, 1990.

Hyde, F.E. *Liverpool and the Mersey*. Newton Abbot, 1971.

Jackson, G. *The History and Archaeology of Ports*. Tadworth, 1983.

Kemp, P. *The Oxford Companion to Ships and the Sea*. Oxford, 1976.

Odin, A. (comp.). *A Bibliography of Nautical Books*. Southampton, 1994.

Paget-Tomlinson, E. *The Illustrated History of Canal and River Navigations*. Sheffield, 1993.

Williams, D.M. and White, A.P. (comps.). *A Select Bibliography of British and Irish Theses about Maritime History, 1792-1990*. St. John's, 1992.

Acknowledgements

The editors would like to acknowledge members of the Archives Department of Merseyside Maritime Museum both past and present for their contributions to this publication. In particular, Dawn Littler, David le Mare, Helen Threlfall, Eileen Edwards, Margaret Evans, Anita Glynn and Paula Larkin must be mentioned, together with Jean Ratcliffe, the Keeper's Secretary at Merseyside Maritime Museum, who typed the final manuscript. Professor Peter Davies of the University of Liverpool and president of the International Maritime Economic History Association; Adrian Jarvis, curator of port history; and Professor Lewis R. Fischer must be thanked for their help, advice and criticism. Finally, we would like to thank the Trustees of National Museums and Galleries on Merseyside and the Council of the IMEHA for supporting this publication. The editors take responsibility for any shortcomings of this guide and welcome any constructive criticism and comment.

CHAPTER 1
RECORDS DEPOSITED OR PRESENTED UNDER THE PUBLIC RECORDS ACTS, 1958

Part 1: Deposited Records

Liverpool Statutory Register of British Merchant Ships

"Of all the shipping records in the United Kingdom, those in Liverpool are the most perfect." R.C. Jarvis, "Liverpool Statutory Registers of British Merchant Ships," *Transactions of the Historic Society of Lancashire & Cheshire*," CV (1953), 107-122.

Until recently the Collector of HM Customs & Excise also acted as Registrar of British Merchant Ships, on behalf of the Registrar of Shipping and Seamen, in all Customs Ports of the British Isles. The series of registers described below contain some that are unique to Liverpool and are complete except for one volume of Plantation Registers between 1773 and 1779. Originally kept in the Liverpool Customs House, these are often called "Customs Registers."

Records

Appointments

Appointments of officers for declarations of ownership, 1899-1916 and 1943-1965.

C/EX/L/1   3 volumes

Wool Act Register

This contains the text of owner's declarations, made under the Act 12 George II (1739) cap. 21, which was particularly concerned to prevent the export of wool from Ireland by non-British vessels. It recorded the vessel's name; home port; date and place of build (sometimes); whether home, foreign or plantation built; rig (or general type of vessel); tonnage; master's name; names of owner or part-owners; and whether taken as a prize or otherwise of foreign build,

1

together with a reference to the circumstances of its seizure or condemnation, and when and where "made free."

C/EX/L/2   1739-1792   1 Volume

Plantation Registers

These contain the text of owner's declarations, under the Act for preventing frauds and regulating abuses in the Plantation Trade (7-8 William & Mary [1695], cap. 22), recording details as above. The early Liverpool slaving and privateering vessels are found in this series. *On account of their fragility these four volumes may not be consulted by the public but microfilms are available in the Reading Room.*

> 1743-1756
> 1755-1765
> 1765-1773
> 1779-1784
> C/EX/L/3/1-4   4 Volumes

Certificate of Registry

Official copies of the certificates of registry, granted under the Registry Act of 26 George III (1786), cap. 60, sec. 3.

C/EX/L/4   1786-1823   38 Volumes

Register Books

These contain the details of ships registered under the above Act with additional details: the owner's residence and occupation; tonnage under the "old measurement" or builder's measurement rule; and a more systematic description of the vessel, length, breadth, and depth (in feet and inches) and number of decks and masts, with particulars of stern configuration and figurehead if any.

C/EX/L/5   1786-1823   12 Volumes

Register Books

These contain the details of ships registered under the Registry Act 4 George IV (1823), cap. 41, including in addition to the above, a reference to the builder's certificate, type of bowsprit etc., the division of the property of the vessel into sixty-four shares, and the allocation and transfer of each share (e.g. sale, inheritance, mortgage, etc.).

C/EX/L/5   1824-1836   13 Volumes

Register Books

These contain the details of ships registered under the Registry Act 5-6 William IV (1836), cap. 56. This changed rates of tonnage and dimension measurement, and is referred to as "new measurement."

C/EX/L/5   1836-1855   27 Volumes

Register Books

The Merchant Shipping Act, 17-18 Victoria (1854), changed the measurement of tonnage by introducing gross and net measurements. Length, breadth and depth of hold rules also changed. Engine-room dimensions, number and nominal horsepower of steam engines are included. This series continues to the present and the deposited registers are "closed," i.e., evidence is provided that all vessels in a particular volume have been re-registered, scrapped or lost at sea. As registers are "closed," they are deposited in the Archives.

C/EX/L/5   1855-1942   55 Volumes

Subsidiary Register Books of Non-Liverpool Registered Vessels

Contain the details in the form of L5/1-12 above, apparently for "calling ships" at Liverpool. It was not statutorily required to be kept and was discontinued in 1818. Some 10,000 vessels were recorded.

C/EX/L/6   1788-1818   10 Volumes

Transaction Books

These contain details of transactions in the descent of ownership (subsequent to first registry) in respect of vessels first registered before 1 May 1855.

C/EX/L/7   c. 1855-1890   13 Volumes

Curve Books

These contain cross sections of vessels to enable the calculation of gross and net tonnage, which were based on internal volume. They are a useful though limited substitute for a lines plan of a vessel. Produced under 17-18 Victoria, cap. 104, sec. 21, Liverpool appears to be the only port where these records survive.

C/EX/L/8	1855-1871	7 Volumes

Fishing Vessels Register

Individual cancelled registers of such vessels, including many from Southport and Wirral.

C/EX/L/9	1921-1925	1 Box

Manchester Registry

Register Book

C/EX/M/1	1894-1915	1 Volume

Runcorn Registry

Note: C/EX/L/4/(79) in the Liverpool registry is a register of vessels passing through Runcorn Dock, 1847-1850.

Register books	1862-1937	2 Volumes	
Admeasurement book	1833-1845	1 Volume	
C/EX/R/1	3 Volumes		
C/EX/R/2	Transaction Books c. 1860-1930		2 Volumes

References

Craig, R. and Jarvis, R. *Liverpool Registry of Merchant Ships*. Manchester, 1967.

MacGregor, D.R. *Fast Sailing Ships*. 2nd ed., London, 1988, 23-25, 97-98, 151-152, 271-272, explains with great clarity the changes of measurement rules.

Part 2: Presented Records

Introduction

The Public Record Office (PRO) from time to time has offered material that is either duplicate − or felt not to be of sufficient *general* national interest − to local or specialist repositories. The Charity Commission's records contained duplicate reports of maritime charities and these will be found in volume 2 (Shipping Charities and educational establishments).

Board of Trade Crew Agreements, Lists and Logs, 1857 Onwards

These are in effect contracts of employment for seamen serving on a particular ship and provide biographical details, position on board, last ship, rate of pay, rations to be issued and conduct on voyage. The log is not a navigational log but a form in which the master can record any incidents affecting crew, such as desertion or discharge through ill-health or death. They were filed by the year of voyage and the official number of the ship. The latter can be found in Lloyd's Register or the Mercantile Navy Lists. Seventy percent of these records are held by the Maritime History Archives, Memorial University of Newfoundland (a microfiche of its holdings is available), ten percent are at the PRO (together with a "celebrated vessels" series), ten percent at the National Maritime Museum, Greenwich, and ten percent in local Record Offices with ports in their areas. The Liverpool City Record Office holds several hundred for Liverpool-registered ships (list available). The Maritime Museum holds photocopies or transcripts of lists and logs for the *Marco Polo* 1851 (D/MKS) and the *Jhelum* 1849 (D/JHE) and about seventy other crew lists and agreements (a few with logs). Some sixty more lists are in the Archives of the British and African Steam Navigation Co. and are noted under that entry (see 4 − shipowners).

Records

P/SL   1863-1910   2 Boxes

Reference

Watts, C.T. and M.J. *My Ancestor was a Merchant Seaman*. London, 1991.

National Dock Labour Board

The National Dock Labour Board was set up in 1947 to solve the prevailing casual labour system in British ports. Its aims were to ensure that dock work was undertaken only by workers registered with local Boards and to improve the regularity of work. In 1967 a revised Dock Workers' Scheme was implemented to give registered dockers permanent employment. This was abolished in 1988. These duplicate minutes were presented in 1993.

Records

Liverpool Local Board, 1948-1989
Garston & Widnes Board, 1952-1965

P/NDLB   1948-1989   18 Volumes

CHAPTER 2
RECORDS OF OFFICIAL ORGANISATIONS
PUBLIC RECORDS ACTS, 1958

The Mersey Conservancy Commission

The Mersey Conservancy Commission was established in 1842 to protect the tidal regime of the Mersey estuary for navigation. Its printed reports are in the Upper Mersey Navigation Commission Archives and the MDHB Collection, section P/2. Much of the MDHB Marine Surveyor's department's correspondence is concerned with the work of the Commission. There are also references in the MDHB's Legal, Worked-Up papers and other managerial papers.

Reference

Mountfield, S. *Western Gateway*. Liverpool, 1965.

The Mersey Docks and Harbour Board, Its Antecedents and Successor

The MDHB, its antecedent's and successor's collection is the Maritime Museum's largest and most important Archives. It covers the history of the port of Liverpool from the eighteenth to the late twentieth century. The Liverpool Town Council was the original port authority. In 1709, it was involved in the promotion of an Act to build the first enclosed dock on the site of the original "Pool" and acted as trustee of the dock estate until 1858. As the port expanded and its management became more complex its affairs were delegated to a committee. This was first mentioned in 1761 and made permanent in 1793, which is the starting date of the minute books. Its powers were enhanced in 1811, but it remained under the control of the Liverpool Corporation. Dock users were first represented on the Committee in 1825. Between 1845 and 1847, permanent sub-committees were set up to cope with the major aspects of port business such as finance, harbour administration and building works.

From about 1850 the Liverpool Corporation came under increasing outside pressure from Parliament, Manchester interests and dock users to relinquish control of the port to a separate public body. This resulted in the establishment of the MDHB in 1858. The Board became the overall port authority for the lower Mersey. It took over the incomplete docks at Birkenhead but not the London and North Western Railway Co.'s dock at Garston.

The Board comprised twenty-four elected members and four nominated by the Mersey Conservancy Commissioners. The Board was served by paid officials, of which the Secretary (re-titled Secretary and General Manager between 1894 and 1963), Treasurer, Solicitor, Harbour Master, Marine Surveyor and Water Bailiff, and Engineer-in-Chief were the most important. An elaborate administrative system developed, including nine standing committees to oversee the work of each major department. The system survived with some changes until 1972 when the Board was transformed into the Mersey Docks and Harbour Company, the present port authority.

The minutes of the Board (proceedings) are continuous from 1858 to 1965. Most of its committees met weekly and their minutes exist in near continuous series until 1958 or 1965, except for the pilotage committee which covers the years 1851-1963. Some meetings of the Board were recorded verbatim between 1867 and 1912. With the addition of records from the departments responsible for legal matters, engineering and estates management, the volume of material exceeds 2300 linear feet.

A short cut into the business of the Board is provided by the "worked-up papers," summaries of decisions and digests of information on specific matters that include such diverse matters as the allocation of berths for shipping companies, staff salaries and smuggling. The large collection of newscuttings, which starts in 1887, is of equal value and makes a good starting point for sixth form, first degree and adult students. It also contains a wide range of information about general commercial matters and port activities.

The MDHB collection incorporates not only written records but also thousands of plans of docks, buildings and ships, and hundreds of photographs. These are supplemented by the South Docks Survey (1982-1984), which carried detailed documentary and field surveys on the history and archaeology of the docks taken over by the Merseyside Development Corporation. This survey work has been continued by the Curator of Port History to cover the docks within the Development Corporation's remit – the Liverpool Central docks from Princes Dock to Sandon Dock and the Birkenhead system – in a series of published monographs. Most are in print and available in the Library. The work of the Mersey Docks & Harbour Co. after 1972 is documented in its annual reports, accounts, guides to the port operations and its *Port News* newspaper.

The reference code *MDHB* has been applied to all the Archives whether they are those of the antecedents or successor of the Board. Many series are continuous throughout. Because of their size and variety, each section has its own subsidiary code under the master code *MDHB*.

Ref. Code

Minutes and proceedings of the Board, the board and
its antecedents; proceedings passed under seal.   M/P

Files of supporting papers.	COM
Discussions at the Board.	DISC
Worked-up papers (bound).	WUP
Worked-up papers (unbound).	WUP/L
Antecedent files.	WUP/LA
Legal papers	LEG
Deeds	D
Estates Departments	EST
Investment Records	INV
Financial Records	FIN
Management Files	M
Reports	R
General Manager's Files	GM
Statistics	S
Operational Records (including Dock Registers)	OP
Book of Rates for Docks and Warehouses	DR
Engineer's Department Records	ENG
Marine Surveyor and Water Bailiff's Records	M/S
Maps, Plans and Drawings	M/D
Wreck Files	W/R
Vessels of MDHB	V
Staff and Wages Records	SW

Uniform of Employees	U
New Head Office at Pier Head	DO
National Dock Labour Board	NDLB
Port Defence	PD
Port Emergency Committee	PEC
Port Labour Committee	PLC
Printed Material	P
Public Relations	PR
Newscuttings (Bound Volumes)	NC
Newscuttings (Unbound)	NC/L
Photographs	PHO
Miscellaneous Volumes	MV
Early Miscellaneous Papers	DT
Pilotage	PIL

Records

Minutes and proceedings of the Board and antecedents, including the Liverpool Borough Council Docks Committee, its sub-Committee, parliamentary audit commissioners, absorbed dock companies, and registers of proceedings under seal.

DOCK COMMITTEE OF LIVERPOOL BOROUGH COUNCIL

From 1793 until 1857 Liverpool Docks were administered by a Committee of Liverpool Borough Council which acted as the Trustee of the Docks Estate. Minute Books: (indexed)

MDHB/MP/1   1784-1857   19 Volumes

Proceedings of Sub-Committees

Sub-Committee of Finance (indexed)
MDHB/MP/2   1846-1857   6 Volumes

Sub-Committee for Department of Harbour and Dock Masters (indexed)
MDHB/MP/3   1847-1857   5 Volumes

Sub-Committee for Department of Marine Surveyor (indexed)
MDHB/MP/4   1847-1857   4 Volumes

Sub-Committee for Master Porters: unsigned (indexed)
MDHB/MP/5   1851-1857   3 Volumes

Sub-Committee for Warehouse Management (indexed)
MDHB/MP/6   1847-1857   7 Volumes

Sub-Committee of Works (indexed)
MDHB/MP/7   1846-1857   4 Volumes

Miscellaneous Sub-Committees of Dock Committee:

Proceedings for purchase of property under the Dock Act of 1825 (index only)
1825-1828; Proceedings for establishing Telegraphic Communication with
Holyhead: 1826-1828; Parliamentary Sub-Committee (indexed): 1845-1857;
Sub-Committee of Queen's Visit: 1851; Battery Sub-Committee (indexed):
1845-1846.

MDHB/MP/8   1825-1857   6 Volumes

Mersey Docks and Harbour Board

Proceedings of the Board (indexed)
MDHB/MP/9   1858-1965   35 Volumes

Proceedings of the Finance Committee (indexed)
This supervised the Treasurer's Department
MDHB/MP/10   1859-1965   55 Volumes

Proceedings of the Parliamentary Committee (indexed)
This convened as required to oversee the preparation of bills and other
parliamentary matters.
MDHB/MP/11   1867-1965   6 Volumes

Proceedings of the Docks and Quays Committee (indexed)
This supervised the Harbour Master's Department.
MDHB/MP/12   1860-1965   34 Volumes

Proceedings of the Marine Committee (indexed)
This supervised the work of the Marine Surveyor which included surveying,
buoys and lights.
MDHB/MP/13   1861-1965   24 Volumes

Proceedings of the Pilotage Committee (indexed)
MDHB/MP/14   1859-1950, 1964-1970   31 Volumes

Liverpool Pilotage Sub-Committee
MDHB/MP/14a   1880-1957   5 Volumes

Proceedings of Master Porters/Traffic Committee (indexed).
Proceedings of Master Porters Committee/Special Meeting of Traffic Commit-
tee, indexed: 1 vol. 1858-1861 & Jan-July 1862. This supervised the work of
the Traffic Manager of which master porterage was a major component.
In 1958 the Traffic Committee merged with the Warehouse Committee.
MDHB/MP/15   1862-1958   36 Volumes

Proceedings of Warehouse committee (indexed)
In 1958 the Warehouse committee was replaced by the Traffic and Warehouse
Committee.
MDHB/MP/16   1858-1958   27 Volumes

Proceedings of the Traffic & Warehouse Committee (indexed)
MDHB/MP/16A   1958-65   1 Volume

Proceedings of Works Committee (indexed)
This supervised the Engineer-in-Chief's department.
MDHB/MP/17   1858-1965   39 Volumes

Miscellaneous Volumes of Proceedings (General) (indexed)
Special Committee & Board Memorandum Book Vol. 1 1887-1912
Special (Railway Traffic) Committee Book 1905-1908
MDHB/MP/18   1887-1912   2 Volumes

Proceedings of the Commissioners appointed by Act of Parliament to inspect,
audit and adjust the accounts of the Trustees of the Liverpool Docks
MDHB/MP/19   1822-1897   5 Volumes

Town Dues Committee
Minutes   1830-1834   1 Volume

Town Dues Sub-Committee
Minutes   1853-1857   1 Volume

MDHB/MP/20

Records of Independent Dock Companies Now Absorbed

Birkenhead Dock Company

Works Committee Draft Minutes: 1845-1851
Parliamentary Committee: 1852
Accounts: 1845-1855

Founded in 1844 to develop Wallasey Pool as an alternative to Liverpool; it ran
into various obstacles and was absorbed into the MDHB in 1858.

MDHB/MP/21   1845-1855   2 Volumes

Herculaneum Dock Company

Draft Minutes

A small private dock in South Liverpool, taken over and rebuilt, 1858-1866.

MDHB/MP/22   1846-1851   1 Volume

Proceedings under Seal

MDHB/MP/23   1860-1948   5 Volumes

Recent Additions

Proceedings of the Board's Staff Committee

MDHB/MP/24   1922-1965   3 Volumes

**Extracts from the Minutes of the Common Council of the Borough of
Liverpool**

MDHB/MP/25   1699-1772   1 Volume

Minutes of the Merchants Commissioners of Audit for the Liverpool Docks

MDHB/MP/26		1738-1857		1 Volume

Files of Supporting Papers

The decisions of the Board and its committees were backed up by reports and information recorded in these files, which are extensive but incomplete.

Board

MDHB/COM/1		1914-1962		5 Boxes

Committees (unless otherwise described, the papers are committee files)

Docks and Quays

Includes correspondence re: proposed transfer of German ships to the British Government at Liverpool, May 1919; poster re: danger of mines on seashore, May 1919.
MDHB/COM/2		258 Boxes

Finance

Miscellaneous papers	1888-1905
Committee files	1914-1948
MDHB/COM/3	c. 200 Boxes

Marine

Miscellaneous papers	
including lifeboat files	1861-1908
Committee files	1914-1965

Includes programme for visit of Grand Duke Michael of Russia, Sept. 1916, and references to vessels striking mines, Aug. 1917.
MDHB/COM/4		172 Boxes

Parliamentary
MDHB/COM/5		1890, 1914-35, 1950-62 13 Boxes

Pilotage
MDHB/COM/6		1885-1966		c. 300 Boxes

Traffic

Master Porterage papers	1860-1884	
Committee files	1913-1961	
MDHB/COM/7	137 Boxes	

Traffic and Warehouse

MDHB/COM/8	1962-1965	7 Boxes

Warehouse

Miscellaneous papers	1863-1908
Committee files	1914-1958
MDHB/COM/9	140 Boxes

Works

Miscellaneous papers	1863-1908
Committee files	1914-1965
MDHB/COM/10	208 Boxes

Discussions at the Board

Discussions at Board Meetings on some matters were recorded verbatim between 1867 and 1912. Up to 1890, they included major policy items such as the acquisition of the Parkhill Estate or the resignation of Alfred Holt in 1884. After 1890, they increased in number and subject matter. The topics are diverse and reveal the variety of opinion within the membership of the Board and its committees. They also frequently shed light upon criticism of the Board from non-members with an interest in its operations.

This is a selection only: Annual Inspection of Lightships 1890; Trade Union Congress given facilities to view docks 1890; Insanitary conditions of Dock Office 1890; Refreshment Rooms – Prince's and George's Landing Stages 1890; Deputations from Liverpool Cotton Association to examine necessity for General Manager 1890; Liverpool Steam Ship Owners Association to examine questions of necessity for General Manager 1890; Minutes re: payment of Cunard Steamship Co. for victualling troops during Dock Labourers Strike 1891; Wearing of "button" by those employed in warehouses 1891; Difficulty in obtaining Correct Returns of Weights of cotton landed at Quays 1891; Funding Board's Debt 1891; Suggested transfer to National Lifeboat Institution of Board's Lifeboats 1891; Lifeboat Station at Formby 1891; Accommodation for Foreign Cattle Trade 1893; Theft of Tobacco Stores in Transit Shed at Hornby Dock 1893; Control of Baggage Porters on Princes Landing Stage 1893; Visit of International Maritime Congress 1893; Articles in Newspapers, Criticism, actions of Board 1893; Proposed purchase of Steam Yacht *Galatea* 1895;

Proposed new cattle market at Bootle c.1895; Liverpool Fruit Trade 1895; Importation of American Cotton into Liverpool & Manchester 1896; Embarkation of Boston Artillery Corps from Princes Landing Stage 1896; Signals used by vessels not under way in fog 1896; Cotton statistics 1896; Visit of Channel Fleet 1898; Proposed powers to make bye-laws as to smoking 1898; Accident to horse on Board Property 1898; Pilotage of Yacht *Jason* (Bibby Family Yacht) 1899; Article Landing and Accommodation for Irish Cattle 1900; Port Defences 1900; Anthracite coal for use of steam winches 1900; Commission allowed by Board's Definition of work "Broker" 1900; Contribution to Dock Yard Worker's Relief Fund 1900; Commission granted to a Merchant 1900; Position of Training Ships in River 1900; Punishment of Pilot for drunkenness 1900; Trial for Motor Wagons 1901; Electric Power for Dock Estate 1901; Death of President of USA 1901; Removal of wrecks from Crosby Channel 1901; Accidental Death of Diver 1902; Superannuation of a Messenger 1902; Establishment of Liverpool University 1902; Import of Maize 1902; Leak in Foundations of New Dock Office 1903; Picture of Liverpool Docks for St. Louis Exhibition 1904; Dismissal of Dock Gateman for taking a bribe from a Flat Master 1904; Opening of new Dock Offices and Cotton Exchange 1906; Erosion of Taylor's Bank 1906; Inspection of Askew Spit 1906.

In addition the following commodity trades are referred to specifically: cattle; salt; cotton; silver; fruit; sugar; grain; tobacco; grapes; timber; maize; tomatoes; rice; and wool.

MDHB/DISC/1-252　　　　　1867-1965　　　　　25 Boxes

Worked-Up Papers

These documents are a unique class, peculiar to the MDHB, and contain a summary of decisions reached by various committees, supported by references to correspondence and other records, some of which have not survived. Many extend over long periods and were used to check precedents on specific topics and policies. The variety of subjects is wide but the quality of information varies. For example, information on shipping companies is largely concerned with minor changes in berths. There are two main series, bound and unbound, the latter is indexed in two manuscript volumes. It is intended to produce a consolidated index of this important series in the near future. A selection of the topics in the bound papers is included to provide an idea of their range.

Bound volumes of worked-up papers:
MDHB/WUP　　　　　c.1850-c.1970　　　　　131 boxes

Unbound files of worked-up papers:
MDHB/WUP/L　　　　　c.1850-c.1970　　　　　98 Boxes

Worked-up Papers – Bound

A
Accidents in various dock departments
Accommodation for coal in Liverpool and Birkenhead
Albert Dock Warehouses
Askew Spit, Taylor's Bank, Dinorben Quarry revetments

B
Barges, *Tamar* and *Tay*
Belfast SS Co Berths
Bidston Dock
Birkenhead Dock Warehouses

C
Canteens, Dock Estate
Cattle Trade Accommodation
Coal Contracts
Coast Line Berths
Cold Storage accommodation
Composite & Corn Warehouses
Crane accommodation and crane charges
Cunard SS Co. Berths

D
Damage to the Board's property
Defences of the Port
Dock Gates
Dock Improvements
Dock Lines of Railways
Dock/Police/schemes/strikes/berthing
Dredging
Dublin SP Co., Belfast SP Co. Berths

E
Elder Dempster Berths
Electric light (Lucigen and Wells lights)
Esparto Grass, Molasses, etc.
Explosive substances

F
Fires, and lights on the Dock Estate
Foreign animals/disease/slaughter houses/refrigerating rooms, wharf lettings

G
Galatea (MDHB Steamer)
George's Dock
Gladstone Dock
Graving Dock Grid Iron Rates and Deposits

H
Harrison, T. & J. Berths
High level coal railway
Hilbre Island
Holt, A. & Co. Berths
Hopper Barges
Huts cocoa vans
Hydraulic machinery

I
Irregularities – Pilotage and warehouse dept.

L
Labour unemployment grants
Lamps, sunlights, mooring posts, slides
Lancashire Plateway
Landing stages, destruction by fire
Lifeboats
Lighthouses
Liverpool grain storage

M
Manchester Ship Canal
Master Porters' Rates
Measure for Tonnage
Mersey Conservancy/Railway/Subway
Moorings – River and Bromborough, tanker

N
New Bye-laws/dock offices/works at the North and South End
Nova Scotia and Mann Island, property shed, Canning Dock

O
Official residences
Overhead Railway

P
PSNC Berths
Petroleum – installations
Pilotage
Pluckington Bank

Q
Quay rents

R
Railway and Canal traffic
Regulations for prevention of collision at sea
Repairs and maintenance – Engineer's Dept.
Runcorn and Garston

S
Sheds and Warehouses (Birkenhead)
Shipbuilding Yards
Steam tugs/winches
Strikes – dock
Surveys

T
Telegraphs on dock estate
Telegraphy, wireless – lightships and lighthouses
Timber Trade Tobacco Accommodation
Towing vessels in Liverpool and Birkenhead docks
Trade committee

U
Uniform clothing

V
Vessels anchoring (in the track of ferry boats)
Vigilant and *Salvor* (MDHB vessels)

W
War
White Star berths
Wool Trade
Wrecks, etc.
Wrecks in docks
MDHB/WUP   c.1850-c.1970   131 Boxes

Antecedent Files

These are a special class of worked-up paper about the life and career of members of the MDHB, usually compiled on their decease. A number of eminent dock electors, merchants or shipowners who paid the dock dues were the subject of such papers. Sir Alfred Jones, Chairman of Elder Dempster, was one example. The career of a Board member was always traced through all his membership of the Board's committees. Many of these papers constitute a full obituary file. They are particularly informative between 1885 and 1920.

MDHB/WUP/LA   c.1861-1970   323 files, 6 boxes

Legal Papers

This large section of the Archives contains papers generated in the course of acquiring and managing property, in applications and representations to Parliament and in litigation. It covers a huge variety of topics, many of them in minute detail. One of its peculiar benefits is that there are often different drafts of the same document, with pencil comments on the earlier draft suggesting why it should be changed. Similarly, we find evidence prepared which was not, in the event, presented and which therefore expands on "the public record" of an application to Parliament or a court case.

The legal papers can fill in important gaps elsewhere in the collection. There is, for example, nothing from the Engineer's Department to reveal how the eighteenth-century river wall was constructed, but when a piece fell down and became the subject of litigation, the legal department had to find out, and the fruits of their labours are in E11, E12 and E13. The only good plan of the Stanley Tobacco Warehouse in the collection was prepared in the course of a dispute over its rating valuation. But details of routine procedures are not usually permanently recorded. For instance, the mechanism for calculating and paying the wages of manual workers was only revealed when a timekeeper defrauded the Board in a rather big way with no less than fifty-two written statements from people involved (Legal E6 and E7).

Sub-section A covers the papers relating to those Bills in Parliament promoted by MDHB or its antecedents. The Board and its antecedents seem to have been almost continually in Parliament seeking fresh powers for further expansion. The value of this material is largely in the mass of evidence, verbal and statistical, presented by the various parties.

Liverpool Dock Bills 1855

These contain information on costs, estimates, water and quay space; correspondence regarding allocation of berths; information on dock duties received from

1752; correspondence re: local charges on shipping, verbatim notes of discussions, plans and a list of all the ports in the world with which Liverpool traded in 1853-1854, including the tonnage carried.
MDHB/LEG/A7   1839-1855   46 Files

Liverpool Town and Dock Dues (St. Helens Canal and Railway)

This bill was intended to relieve traffic using the Garston and Widnes docks and the Sankey Canal of Liverpool Port Dues. The bundle includes petitions, briefs, etc., from the Dock Trust and evidence given in Parliament.
MDHB/LEG/A9   1857   7 Files

Mersey Conservancy and Dock Bill 1857

This bill contains a private letter re: mismanagement of Birkenhead Docks. References to payment of dues by vessels unloading in the River.
MDHB/LEG/A12   1847-1857   40 Files

MDHB (Money) Bill 1859

Contains an account of vessels entering through the Sandon Basin during 1853 and 1854. Reference to the *City of Washington*'s record passage from New York to Liverpool in eleven days. References to timber trade and dock fines.
MDHB/LEG/A22   1854-1859   33 Files

MDHB Bill 1862

References to Graving Dock accommodation.
Numerous petitions in Parliament for and against Bill.
Reference to Pilotage.
MDHB/LEG/A25   1860-1862   37 Files

MDHB Bill (1864)
Proposed mode of measuring ships by new Merchant Shipping Bill; number and tonnage of ships trading between Liverpool and ports *within the limits of Confederate States of America* (1863); application to Parliament for bill enabling MDHB to expand the docks to accommodate new lines of steamers (1863); total number of sailing vessels with their tonnage that have entered/left port of Liverpool for foreign parts 1845-1863; London and North Western Railway Bill; tonnage of timber; total number of steamers and sailing vessels left port for previous fifteen years.

MDHB/LEG/A28   1850-1869   69 Files

MDHB Bill 1871
Includes plan of approaches to Liverpool landing stage and proposed improvements; pamphlets re: improved ferry and river approaches; plan for closing George's dock basin and converting it into a wet dock.
MDHB/LEG/A37   1860-1863   63 Files

MDHB Overhead Railway Bill 1878
Proposals for overhead railway with petitions, evidence, estimates, etc.
MDHB/LEG/A47   1877-1878   24 Files

MDHB Bill 1881
Extracts from minute books of Pilotage Committee, 1779-1875; extracts from proceedings of Pilotage Sub-Committee appointed to consider the subject of pilot boat ownership; list of Liverpool pilot boats including details of size and costs 1881; authorisation of MDHB to acquire and work vessels for pilotage service.
MDHB/LEG/A49   1779-1881   28 Files

MDHB (Overhead Railway) Bill 1882
Contains photos of models.
MDHB/LEG/A50   1877-1885   33 Files

MDHB (Various Powers) Bill 1893
Contains statements regarding coasting lines and handbills advertising North Wales Steam Packets Cos., viz the Aberystwyth and Aberdovey Steam Packet Cos. and Portmadoc and Pwllheli Steam Packet Cos.
MDHB/LEG/A57   1870-1893   42 Files

MDHB Bill 1895
Statements: re: vessels carrying cattle into Liverpool 1880 and 1894; length of time during which cattle remain in lairage on foreign animals wharves at Liverpool before slaughter; particulars of accommodation for foreign animals; bill to authorise construction of floating landing stage.
MDHB/LEG/A59   1892-1895   47 Files

General Papers re: MDHB (Canada Street Works)
Includes papers re: Irish cattle trade, landing stage and coal shipments to Birkenhead.
MDHB/LEG/A73   1898-1901   37 Files

MDHB Bill 1903
Contains tonnage relating to various ships; grain trade; statistics re: performance of steamers; brochures of Cunard, White Star and Hamburg America Lines.
MDHB/LEG/A77   1903-1905   15 Files

Papers re: Dock Strikes, 1911 and 1914
Includes report of Special Committee of City of Liverpool re: intimidation
during trade disputes; picketing; newscuttings, handbills; appointment of special
constables, etc.
MDHB/LEG/A94   1906-1914   22 Files

MDHB Bill 1936 (Correspondence Folders)
Position of MDHB in Port of Liverpool re: seaplanes 1935; list of barges sunk
in MDHB's docks from 1925 to 1935.
MDHB/LEG/A103   1906-1936   7 Files
                                                87 Boxes in All

Sub-section B is concerned with the Board's representations in Parliament
relating to local government legislation in the Merseyside region and adjoining
areas. Lists of many of the bundles are available in the reading room.
MDHB/LEG/B   c.1864-1897   47 Boxes

Sub-section C is concerned with the Board's representations in Parliament
relating to the various railway bills. Lists of many of the bundles are available
in the reading room.
MDHB/LEG/C   c.1858-1933   49 Boxes

Sub-section D covers the papers relating to the Mersey pilotage service and its
relationship with the MDHB. The Board was seeking to take over the pilotage
service and succeeded in doing so in 1882. Other material concerns disciplinary
proceedings and pilots' uniforms.

Pilotage (Compulsory) Abolition Bill 1871
Includes a list of Liverpool Pilot Boat Owners, 1870; copies of the bill; various
petitions against the bill.
MDHB/LEG/D3   1849-1871   1 Box

Printed Returns by the Board of Trade
Showing gross earnings of apprentices during 1872.
MDHB/LEG/D4   1874   1 Box

Purchase of Pilot Boats by the Board
Includes a list of masters and mates holding Liverpool pilotage certificates on
1 June, annually, since 1860; memo re: pilot boat share prices, 1882; return
showing age and depreciation of pilot boats, 1881; proposed purchase of pilot
boats, 1881; memo re: instruction to purchase pilot boats, 1882.
MDHB/LEG/D6&7   1854-1883   1 Box each

Little v. The Board; Pilot's Appeal from Decision of the Pilotage Committee
Includes extracts from log of No. 9 pilot boat; statements of what passed at committee meeting, 1892, re: No. 5 pilot boat touching Middle Mouse Island.
MDHB/LEG/D13   1887-1892   1 Box

Proposed Pilots' Uniform
Includes examples of other buttons and badges and local by-laws.
MDHB/LEG/D17   1875-1908   1 Box

Martin v. MDHB (Appeal of pilot from decision of Pilotage Committee re: 1894 Merchant Shipping Act, Section 610)
Includes extracts from Pilotage Character Book re: J.R. Martin; reports of irregularities, e.g., "missed boat," "drunk."
MDHB/LEG/D18   1887-1905   1 Box
                                                14 Boxes in All

Sub-section E covers the papers relating to prosecutions and court cases in which the MDHB was involved. A variety of subjects are covered, including pollution, the Mersey Tunnel, shipwrecks, fraud and compensation.

Rex v. John Joseph Lynch and John Rous re: Wages Frauds in the Engineer's Department, 1902
Includes handwritten letter from J.J. Lynch from his prison cell at Walton Jail, Liverpool, giving a detailed account of the manner in which he carried out the frauds. Mentions blackmail Nov. 1902.
MDHB/LEG/E6&E7   1882-1904   1 Box each

Prosecution of W.K. Earle, Manager of Hutchinsons Estate, Widnes
Action of Mersey Conservancy Commission for depositing rubbish on shore of River Mersey, as liable to be washed into the river (Dec. 1910).
MDHB/LEG/E8   1903-1911   1 Box

Sinking of Formby lightship *Planet* on 13 August 1921 by SS *Greenbrier* (Elders and Fyffes Ltd.)
Includes proofs of witnesses, photograph of collision, chart of Liverpool Bay; statement of claim; depositions.
MDHB/LEG/E9   1921-1923   1 Box

John Ferguson (Plaintiff) v MDHB (Defendant) Re: Claim for Balance of Wages during War Service
Includes correspondence and legal documents on the claim. Newspaper cuttings from the *Liverpool Post* and *Mercury*.
MDHB/LEG/E10   1915-1927   1 Box

MDHB (Plaintiff) v. Mersey Tunnel Joint Committee Re: Claims for Damage in Respect of Collapse of River Wall at Georges Dock/Pier Head
Includes correspondence, plans, geological reports and photographic evidence.

MDHB/LEG/E11,12&13	1899-1932	1 Box each
MDHB/LEG/E		10 Boxes in all

Sub-section F comprises papers relating to conveyances and exchanges of land.

MDHB and Manchester Ship Canal re: Tolls on Goods Passing through the cut from Stanley Dock leading to Leeds-Liverpool Canal
Correspondence between MDHB and Bridgewater Navigation Co., Manchester Ship Canal Co., and trustees of the late Duke of Bridgewater; also legal papers re: Leeds and Liverpool Canal v. Manchester Ship Canal Co.

MDHB/LEG/F12	1858-1891	1 Box

J.W. Cropper and Others to MDHB: re: Conveyance of Dingle Bank Estate, Liverpool
Particulars, conditions of sale and plan of Dingle Bank Estate; Correspondence from Earl of Sefton; Dock Engineer's Survey and abstract of title to premises in Toxteth Park.

MDHB/LEG/F17	1809-1887	1 Box

MDHB to Captain Edward Cole and Charles B. Burrow re: Conveyance of Lower and Upper Hoylake Lighthouses
Plan of Lower Hoylake Lighthouse and area, correspondence re: sale of lighthouses, MDHB to Hoylake Sailing Club refusing to purchase land.

MDHB/LEG/F32	1909	1 Box

Purchase of East Side of Queen's Dock by MDHB
Corporation of Liverpool re: lease of property, correspondence re: land, abstracts of titles, plan of East Queen's Dock Quay.

MDHB/LEG/F35	1869-1888	1 Box

Coburg Dock, East Side – Purchase by Board of Properties (1890)
Legal papers, plans of land and register of property re: purchase of land for overhead railway.

MDHB/LEG/F59	1887-1891	1 Box

Exchange of Land between MDHB and Mersey Tunnel Joint Committee
Correspondence re: exchange of land on east side of Morpeth branch dock, plan of Woodside ventilation station building and Mersey Tunnel.

MDHB/LEG/F72	1933-1934	1 Box

Conveyance of George's Dock land to Liverpool Corporation
Correspondence, agreements and memos between Liverpool Corporation and
MDHB. Plans of George's Dock Site, Pier Head River Wall and various Pier
Head sites. Also folder re: pumping of George's Dock.
MDHB/LEG/F/84   1871-1927   1 Box
                                                    32 Boxes in All

Sub-section G contains copies of by-laws and supporting papers. Lists of the
documents in this section are available in the reading room.
MDHB/LEG/G   c.1863-1937   10 Boxes

Sub-section H contains a wide variety of material on a very diverse range of
subjects. Subjects range from eighteenth-century cases and opinions of counsel
to World War II regulations and damage to property. It contains some of the
most interesting documents in the whole Archives, of which only a selection is
described below.

Cases and Opinions of Counsel
These are papers produced in respect of legal actions involving the Trust or the
Board. Subjects include purchase of land, preservation of the Mersey navigation,
Liverpool Dock Bills, By-laws, etc.
MDHB/LEG/H9-15   1762-1894   c.209 Items

Reports Compiled by John Rennie, Civil Engineer
Produced for a scheme to extend and improve the Port of Liverpool, consisting
of a report giving detailed plans and costings; a second report streamlining the
first and an estimated costing for an additional basin north of Prince's Dock.
MDHB/LEG/H16   1809-1811   3 Items

Liverpool Corporation v. Bolton et al. re: Town Dues
Includes a report of local charges on shipping; brief for the Corporation; details
of Birkenhead Dock Bills (management and construction); appendices produced
for the case including correspondence and documents produced in evidence;
extracts from the Town Books (1551-1726): translation of Charter of King John
to Liverpool (ms.) 1207; contemporary ms. copies of Liverpool Bills of Entry
1763-1791; reports of proceedings, brief for defendants, evidence of witnesses,
judgements, etc.
MDHB/LEG/H17-24   c.1207-1857   11 Boxes

Dock Police Officers
Evidence of the Superintendent of Dock Police, before a committee of the House
of Commons. Includes minutes of Dock Sub-Committee, statistics of offenders.
MDHB/LEG/H25   1836   10 Items

Printed Report of Finance Committee of Liverpool Town Council
This gave rise to the Albert Dock and includes information on other docks and
warehouses on quays, etc.
MDHB/LEG/H26   1839   1 Volume

Telegraph Stations
Correspondence, draft leases, agreements and plans, etc., re: telegraph stations
along the north Wales coast to Anglesey.
MDHB/LEG/H27   1834-63   1 Box

Birkenhead Dock Act
Minutes of a Special Committee re: the Act.
MDHB/LEG/H30   1855-1858   1 Volume

Case: Owners of the *Sierra Nevada* v. Trustees of Liverpool Docks
The *Sierra Nevada* came aground when entering the Wellington half-tide dock
carrying a cargo of guano. The owners of the cargo claimed that the vessel had
caught on a mud bank in the dock, while the trustees claimed that it was sagging
in the middle. A second case was fought by the owners of the *Sierra Nevada*,
and after a long and complicated battle both cases were heard together in the
House of Lords. Contains a wide range of legal papers, including briefs for
defendants, evidence of witnesses, affidavits and correspondence.
MDHB/LEG/H32-34   1855-1868   c.100 Items

Case: Sir Samuel Morton Peto Bt., Thomas Brassey and Others v. MDHB
Peto and Brassey were civil engineers who built railways, docks and bridges all
over the world. An action was fought with the MDHB over the drawing off of
water from Wallasey Pool near the firm's Canada Works, Birkenhead, where
work, including locomotives for the Grand Trunk Railway of Canada and
elsewhere, was being carried out, on the ground that premises had to be
relocated and goods shipped via Liverpool, thus causing a year's profits to be
lost. Includes opinions of counsel, brief of defendants, proceedings, plans,
inventory of plant and stock and other legal papers.
MDHB/LEG/H35   1853-1862   50 Items

**Statements of All Legal Proceedings re: Title of the Crown to Bed or Shores
of the Sea or Tidal Navigable Rivers**
MDHB/LEG/H36   1830-1857   1 File

Mooring of Vessels in Ferry Tracks
Includes memorial of 161 residents of Cheshire to Pilots Committee asking its
members not to anchor between Seacombe and Woodside ferry; By-laws;

MDHB memorials; correspondence; details of collisions of Woodside ferry boats; Special Committee reports, etc.
MDHB/LEG/H37   1853-1878   50 Items

Upper Mersey Dues Bill 1860
Includes minutes of evidence, House of Commons; Petitions of MDHB; correspondence, etc.
MDHB/LEG/H/38

Purchase of the Sandon Works of Messrs. Edward Bury and James Kennedy by the Board (later H.M. Lawrence and Co.)
The sale of the Sandon Works of Sefton Street, Liverpool, in 1863 led to the production of an extensive inventory/catalogue which provides a useful list of the fittings, plant, machinery and stock of a Liverpool shipyard sold as a going concern. The sale catalogue in particular includes detailed descriptions, such as Lot 651 – "The Wrought Iron Keel for a 1,500 Ton ship, drilled and jointed." Other documents include schedules of title deeds, correspondence and surveyors' estimates of the value of the site, etc. (NB: Part of sale catalogue is reproduced in the NMGM's *Ships and Seafarers in the 19th Century* education pack).
MDHB/LEG/H44   1844-1864   1 Box

Printed Volume: Evidence taken before the Marine Committee under an appointment of the Board into the necessity for the establishment of a River Police and to report thereon to the Board (153 pp.)
Contains evidence of pilots, chaplains, police, "overlookers" (for shipping companies), head constable, chairman of Mercantile Marine Association, town clerk, Superintendent of Outdoor Staff, Sailors' Home, Marine Surveyor. (An indexed photocopy is available on request. This will normally be supplied to searchers, not the original).
MDHB/LEG/H45   2 Apr. 1863   1 Volume

Seacombe River Wall
Includes a Report by James Walker, C.Eng., correspondence, and a copy of the agreement of the landowners at Seacombe on the building of the wall. Also includes a letter and report by John B. Hartley, dock engineer, re: the effect of tidal action upon the Cheshire shore north of Seacombe, etc.
MDHB/LEG/H46   1855-1861   24 Items

Case: Co-operative Wholesale Society Ltd v. MDHB
Correspondence re: dues charged at Garston on goods inward and outward. Also legal papers and correspondence, etc.
MDHB/LEG/H75   1887-1890   22 Items

Case: MDHB v Birkenhead Corporation
The action concerned the responsibility for repairs to the Woodside ferry chains.
Includes correspondence between plaintiffs' and defendants' solicitors; affidavits;
plan of Woodside landing stage; and judgement of the Court of Appeal.
MDHB/LEG/H77   1857-1889   57 Items

**Engineering Survey of the River Mersey: – Erection of Tide Gauges and
Survey Marks by the Board**
Contains correspondence and agreements between the Board and Charles J.W.
Blundell of Freshfield, Formby, and Miss Adelaide Watt of Speke for the
erection of survey marks on their property. Also documents and correspondence
re: the extension of J.H. Turner's Engineering survey and a copy of Turner's
report.
MDHB/LEG/H78   1889-1892   3 Files & 9 other Items

Appointment of General Manager: – Report of Special Committee
Includes handwritten and printed opinions of members of the Board on the
feasibility of the appointment; letters to the press; copies of an editorial from the
Journal of Commerce and *Liverpool Courier*; copies of the report of the Special
Committee, etc.
MDHB/LEG/H80   1890-1891   7 Items

**Board of Agriculture Inquiry re: Proposed Foreign Animal Wharves at
Manchester and Salford**
Includes a transcript of notes of proceedings of the Inquiry; MDHB By-laws for
regulating, governing and managing stages, etc., for landing of foreign animals
on its land. Statements showing condition of Woodside and Wallasey lairages,
etc., and details of town dues and dock rates chargeable on cattle landed at
Birkenhead.
MDHB/LEG/H83   1885-1893   23 Items

Bidston Hill – Board's Right of Way and Drainage
Includes correspondence and extracts from conveyance of Bidston Lighthouse
from Robert Vyner Esq. to the trustees. Also a copy release re: the lighthouse
at Little Meols.
MDHB/LEG/H86   1827-1900   3 Items

Depositing of Rubbish on New Ferry Beach
Information against Thirkell and Co. and Robert Smith in the case heard at the
Police Court, Birkenhead, concerning the breaking up of vessels on New Ferry
Beach. Includes briefs, memorandums and lists of vessels being broken up
(1894-1896).
MDHB/LEG/H88   1894-1897   10 Items

Revision of Beaufort Scale
Consisting of correspondence between MDHB and the Meteorological Office,
etc. Includes report of the Director of the Meteorological Office.
MDHB/LEG/H89   1862-1906   5 Items

**Miscellaneous Plans, Documents and Notes re: Liverpool Landing Stages
and Bridges**
Includes plan of Liverpool landing stage; memorandum re: pedestrian bridge at
Ferry landing stage; traffic statistics using Prince's Stage and Riverside Station;
list of dues payable under the Southampton Harbour Act (1903) at Royal Pier.
MDHB/LEG/H90   1902-1907   14 Items

MDHB and Messrs. W. Brown: – Contract for New Dock Office
Includes instructions for competing architects with schedule of requirements;
memorandum of agreement for the construction of the office with William
Brown and Son on the SW portion of George's Dock, Liverpool; contracts, etc.
MDHB/LEG/H95   1897-1903   16 Items

**Wrecks of Various Vessels: – Distribution of Balance of Proceeds of Sales
of Vessel and Cargo**
Consists of solicitors' correspondence re: vessels, includes an agreement
between MDHB and owners, etc., of the steel screw steamer *Avon* re: its
collision with SS *Boynton*.
MDHB/LEG/H130   1916-1921   3 Items

Defence of the Realm Regulations as to Coal and Lighting
Includes maps of railway sidings; statistics of consumption of electricity, gas and
coal; report on fuel and lighting order (1918) and correspondence, etc.
MDHB/LEG/H132   1908-1920   16 Items

General Strike
Includes correspondence, news cuttings, etc.
MDHB/LEG/H144   1926   1 File

World War II
These include correspondence, regulations, dock solicitor's reports on War Acts;
details of casualties, and property damaged, etc.
MDHB/LEG/H148-151   1919-1952   c. 55 Items
MDHB/LEG/H   76 Boxes in All

Sub-section K includes statistical evidence showing progressive history and the
leading changes in ownership and value of land on the north side of Wallasey
Pool including the Seacombe pottery and foundry. There is also a bill of entry

for *Falcon* bound for Shanghai, and papers re: the appointments of managers of the Bowling Iron Company, Bradford, under its Act of Parliament at the Annual General Meeting, as well as details of an Act for confirming and carrying into effect an arrangement made by the Court of Chancery for granting certain powers to the Bowling Iron Company.

MDHB/LEG/K7   1830-1864   58 Items

Proceedings in Arbitration Between Bibby and Co. and MDHB
MDHB/LEG/K13   1861   4 Bound Volumes

Ownership of Land at Birkenhead
Copies of licence, confirmation, *quo warranto* to prior and convent of Birkenhead to build houses at Birkenhead Ferry; transcripts of grant to Ralph Worsley; copy of lease of "Ferry house" at Woodside, abstract of title of Corporation of Liverpool to land and shore in Birkenhead, supplemental proofs re: anchorage charges, correspondence between Dock Liverpool and Seacombe Copper Mills.

MDHB/LEG/K14   1317-1865   86 Documents

Great Western Railway and London and North Western Railway and Board
Map of proposed temporary accommodation for Birkenhead Railway Companies during progress of dock works; map showing goods stations and dock lines; letter from Board of Trade re: barque *Gayhead* and a list of flats employed by Joseph Williams in carrying guano to Liverpool. Traffic statements for fifteen months, 1859, 1860 and 1862.

MDHB/LEG/K19   1855-1975   37 Items

GWR and LNWR and the Board – Arbitration of claim for compensation
London and North Western, Great Western and Birkenhead Railway Companies versus MDHB – transcript of shorthand notes taken.

MDHB/LEG/K20   1864-1865   10 Items

Denton v. Board – Ratings Briefs, etc.
This section includes transcripts of Pipe Rolls, 1228-30, Warrant for making a stone wall around Toxteth Park, 1401. Permission for Gilbert de Haywoode to have two fat bucks of the king's deer in Toxteth Park, 1401, and for Isabella de Stanley to have twelve oaks for timber from Toxteth Park, 1407, a Grant of Office of Parker of Toxteth Park, 1423, a licence to Robert Lawrence to take, in season, one deer in the park, 1423, a Demise to Sir Thomas Stanley and Sir Richard Molyneux of herbage and pannage in Toxteth Park, 1438, and Ministers Accounts, 1641-1642.

MDHB/LEG/K21   1228-1868   51 Items

Liverpool Corporation and the Board – Arbitration re: Purchase by Board of River Craft Dock
Copy of lease of tobacco warehouse, 1865; tobacco warehouse receipts and expenditure, 1857-1875; Ellacott's Statement re: River Craft Dock, 1875; particulars of River Craft Dock Estate, 1876: notes on rates on ships, goods, tobacco, at River Craft and Kings Docks, 1876; statement showing results of earnings, expenditure and surplus, 1865-1875, in tobacco warehouse; statement of receipts and expenditure re: tobacco warehouses; tobacco trades sampling of tobacco rules; block plan of Wapping warehouses; plans for River Craft Dock.
MDHB/LEG/K28   1856-1885   70 Items

Rating of Woodside and Wallasey Lairages, Birkenhead Borough Quarter Sessions, Briefs, Proofs and General Papers
Includes statement of accounts for Wallasey and Woodside Wharves.
MDHB/LEG/K37   1881-1989   83 Items

Rating of Woodside and Wallasey Lairages, Birkenhead Borough Quarter Sessions
Transcript, 5 and 6 Jan. 1898, and Judgement of Recorder, 25 March 1898.
MDHB/LEG/K38   1879-1898   4 Items

Rating of Woodside and Wallasey Lairages, Chester Quarter Sessions, QBD and Ct. of Appeal
Briefs, proofs of evidence and general papers.
MDHB/LEG/K39   1899   36 Items

George's Dock Arbitration, Correspondence, etc.
Includes correspondence re: ferry traffic, etc.; George's Dock and correspondence re: George's Dock steamship returns with First Day's Proceedings re: Case, George's Dock Arbitration, Board v. Liverpool Corporation.
MDHB/LEG/K44   1895-1899   22 Items

George's Dock Arbitration, General Papers
Trade increases in the years 1872-1897, with photo and drawing of the new White Star Offices, James Street, and imports table (wines and spirits), 1881, 1891, 1898. Surveyor's notes and sketches re: proposed George's Dock site.
MDHB/LEG/K45   1893-1901   81 Items

1900 – Duke's Dock Arbitration Purchase by Board from Manchester Ship Canal Co. Plans used in connection with Arbitration
Includes plan showing greatest average and least extension of Pluckington Bank, with plan of bank, showing least, greatest and average areas.
MDHB/LEG/K52   1899   25 Items

1929 Income Tax on Government Grants; Works for the Relief of Unemployment, Correspondence
Includes unemployment grants, committee correspondence and *Times* Law Reports.
MDHB/LEG/K72   1924-1934   6 Items

1929-31 De-rating of Board's Warehouses in Liverpool and Bootle
Includes eight copy documents used in Appeal Court hearing in connection with importation of tobacco, East India wool, sugar and wine.
MDHB/LEG/K74   1931   25 Items

De-rating of Board's Warehouses in Liverpool and Bootle. General, Graphs used before Quarter Sessions; Reproductions of Documents (1929-31)
Includes copies of documentation re: transport and landing of sugar, wool and tobacco at Liverpool Docks, with bills of lading.
MDHB/LEG/K76   1927-1931   2 Items

1929-1931 De-rating of Board's Warehouses in Liverpool and Bootle (General Miscellaneous Papers)
Includes graph of wheat prices, Liverpool Corn Trade Association Ltd. from Clearing House committee's quotations, and appellants' case statement at County Quarter Sessions re: Rating Appeal, West Derby Assessment Area Revenue Officer (Appellants) v. West Derby Liverpool Assessment Committee and Liverpool Grain Storage and Transit Co. Ltd. (Respondents) with the Court of Appeal's opinion on Wool, Wapping, Albert and Stanley Warehouses.
MDHB/LEG/K77   1928-1932   67 Items

De-rating of Board's Warehouses in Liverpool and Bootle (General Correspondence and Newspaper Extracts)
Includes tables showing tonnage stored at Albert Dock, Stanley Dock, Wapping Dock, Wool Warehouse, Waterloo Grain Warehouse, and Brocklebank Warehouse during 1928, as well as a postcard of the port of London's floating crane, *London Mammoth*.
MDHB/LEG/K78   1928-1932   5 Items
MDHB/LEG/K   64 Boxes in All

Sub-section M contains copies of reports, correspondence and other papers concerning Merchant Shipping Bills, shipping codes and other related subjects. Lists of this sub-section are available in the reading room.
MDHB/LEG/M   c.1869-1931   14 Boxes

Sub-section N contains correspondence and papers concerning the Upper Mersey Navigation Commission (UMNC) and the Manchester Ship Canal Bills. Lists of this section are available in the reading room.

MDHB/LEG/N   c.1876-1950   50 Boxes

Deeds

This series is expected to expand in the next instalment of Dock Company records. At present deeds relating to the Herculaneum copper works, pottery and dock are held.

MDHB/D   1772 - c. 1865   4 Boxes

Estates Department

These records are varied, and it is difficult to understand how many came to be so classified. Perhaps it was because of the need for strong-rooms, especially made to hold its deeds and leases, and so other departments also used this facility. The formal estate documents are classified as leases, contracts and agreements. They, and the miscellaneous files, are divided, according to old county boundaries; Lancashire and Cheshire. There is also some Welsh and Scottish material relating to the Board's properties and activities outside Merseyside. They cover all aspects of its operations.

Cheshire Agreements

Refer to tenancy of dock buildings and premises, closures, signal stations, tolls and occupancy of house on Hilbre Island. Seaforth Welding Company and repair of ships at Birkenhead Graving Docks (from 1981).

MDHB/EST/1   1850 - 1981   5 Boxes

Cheshire Contracts

Refer to building of docks, supply of coal, dock machinery, hire of horses, and include significant items: – T. Vernon to build Woodside and Birkenhead Landing Stages, 1860 and 1861/2. T. Brassey to build two camels (for lifting), 1871; Bowdler, Chaffer and Co. to build Steam Paddle Vessel and Dredging machine, 1875.

MDHB/EST/2   1850 - 1955   4 Boxes

Cheshire Leases

Refer to Hilbre Island, land on or near Birkenhead Docks, Dock Warehouses, and include three significant items: – Birkenhead Dock Co. to John Laird 1853 and (from MDHB) 1861, to Cammell Laird of land at Tranmere with detailed plans of works, 1900.

MDHB/EST/3   1850 - 1969   5 Boxes

Lancashire Agreements
Refer to land, railway lines, warehouses, alterations to docks and buildings; utilities and river moorings for Cunard Steamship Co.; Training Ship *Conway*; also refer to new dock engineer; supply of new vessels and wreck removal.
MDHB/EST/4   1839 - 1970   13 Boxes

Lancashire Contracts
Refer to the supply of uniforms, dock works, coal, stationary vessels, removal of wrecks, dock fittings, machinery, lightships, utilities and significantly: — R. and J. Evans for steam screw tug *Hodgson* (with plan), 1882; W.H. Potter, for steam watch vessel, 1884; R. and J. Evans, for iron lightship, 1885; Brundrit and Co., Runcorn, for wooden lightship (with plan) 1886.
MDHB/EST/5   1851 - 1950   10 Boxes

Lancashire Leases
Land for new docks, tenancy of buildings, including a lease (1800) referring to the "Old Wet Dock, Liverpool" using a plan dated 1751, other documents dated 1800-1812, showing elevation of house and warehouse, subject of the lease. Sites for telegraph signal stations, lighthouses, lifeboat stations, consular offices, shipbuilding and ship repair yards: — Charles Grayson, 1824; Peter Cato, 1845; William Rennie, 1849; James Brook, 1851; Thomas Brandeth, 1854; T. Vernon and Son, 1855; W.H. Potter, 1866; Thomas Royden and Sons, 1868.
MDHB/EST/6   1719 - 1972   15 Boxes

Lancashire Miscellaneous
These refer to or include technical drawings, guarantees, Board of Trade certificates, bills of lading, creation of the Port of Manchester, notices to stockholders, wreck salvage, dock buildings, Mersey Bay Project.
MDHB/EST/7   1850 - 1963

Scottish Documents
Refer to the supply of granite refuse.
MDHB/EST/8   1832 - 1903   1 Box

Welsh Documents
Refer to supply of stone from quarries, accommodation for pilots at Point Lynas landing at Amlwch, telegraph stations.
MDHB/EST/9   1779 - 1939   1 Box

Indemnities
Payment of dues on vessels, damage, recovery of wrecks, goods in storage and in transit, including examples of bills of lading with references to named vessels.
MDHB/EST/10   1872 - 1965   11 Boxes

Investments Records

These are unlisted and mostly unsorted. Most are mid-nineteenth century, and a series of registers of bonds is fairly complete.

MDHB/INV   1863-1914   approx. 70 Volumes

Financial Records

This section is not yet fully catalogued. Manuscript notes regarding the early financial situation can be found in MDHB/DT and MDHB/LEG.

Printed Annual Reports and Accounts

Between 1963 and 1969 these were accompanied by detailed reviews, containing some twenty pages of text with illustrations and copious statistics. Significant developments in port activity were highlighted under the headings of shipping, cargo operations, port progress, port publicity, etc. Trade statistics were analysed under various trading areas, imports, exports, commodities and receiving and supplying countries.

MDHB/FIN/1   1755 To Date   7 Boxes

Between 1966-1968 special reports were prepared by the Board's principal accountant. During the 1960s and 1970s the port passed through a financial crisis. The Board finances were restructured. These special reports were highly confidential, shedding light on the run-up to the restructuring. They can only be consulted with the Dock Company's permission at present.

MDHB/FIN/2   1966 - 1968   4 Volumes

The ledgers begin in 1814 and continue to the present; they are not yet sorted.

MDHB/FIN/3   1814 onwards   c.100 Volumes

Volume entitled "Account of the Receipts and Expenditure of the Dock and Light Duties of the Port of Liverpool as Annually Exhibited to Parliament and Delivered to the Trustees, Relating to Princes and Brunswick Dock."

MDHB/FIN/4   1811 - 1859   1 Volume

Cash Book, 1795

Contains the dock dues paid by each vessel and the port from which it came.

MDHB/FIN/5   1 Volume

Management Files

The port endured increasing competition from European and British ports, especially after 1920. The Board's general managers and senior staff travelled widely to gather information, promote the product, reassure existing customers and establish new trade links. The newscuttings files also contain information on the activities of Liverpool's competitors and partners. Files exist for trade with Australia, 1943-1952; Lancashire and Merseyside Industrial Development Association 1967-1968; Ship to Shore Radio, 1943-1948; Floating Plant, 1941-1977 (including photos of launching of *Salvor, Mersey No. 40* and *Atlas*); Radar, 1944-1968; Chairman's papers of Steering Committee on Merseyside Traffic and Transport, 1962-1968; Tranmere Oil Terminal Shipping Programmes 1965-1970; Files on visits abroad, beginning with Lionel A.P. Warner, General Manager, to USA and Canada, 1920, ending with Edward Hughes, Chief Warehouse Manager, visit to America 1963 (other visits include Australia, New Zealand, South Africa, Rotterdam, USA and Canada regarding pallets and mechanical handling, opening of St. Lawrence Seaway, conference on Oil Pollution, Copenhagen); Chairman's files, including annual statements and official hospitality 1950-1963; strikes, 1945-1955; centenary events, 1958.

MDHB/M   1941 - 1968   21 Boxes

Reports

This series of printed reports is clearly only a fraction of those that were actually made to the Board. Many other reports may be found in Worked Up Papers, Legal files, Committee files and especially in the records of the Engineer's Department.

Proposed Dock Extension
Vol 1: Minutes, Report of Special Committee to consider further accommodation for trade — evidence from various trades 1872.
Vol 2: Report of Debate with statistics and plans 1872.

Proposed New Liverpool Port
Report by Engineers 1965

Interim Development of Birkenhead Dock System
First and Second Interim Feasibility Reports 1966, 1967.
MDHB/R   1846-1872; 1965-1967   1 Box

General Manager's Files

These relate to a wage increase for all categories of workers in the docks and give details of awards from employers' organisations; also to proposed alterations to the Stanley Dock tobacco warehouses; congestion at the landing stage and berthing of ferries; papers, reports and booklets from overseas visits.
MDHB/GM   1906 - 1959   6 Boxes

Statistics

These statistics were compiled by the Principal Accountant's Department from returns by stevedores, master porters and others and relate to ships and cargoes. Each monthly statistic summarises the number and net register tonnage of vessels completing discharge or loading, giving the names of vessels, shipping company, principal cargoes, loading berths and number of working days. The summaries also give the number of foreign-going vessels (excluding tankers) using MDHB docks, method of transport, trans-shipment of cargo and countries from which or to which cargoes, other than bulk oil and livestock, were shipped. The tonnage of commodities was broken down into three principal classifications: Foreign-going ships (excluding tankers), tankers and coastwise ships. Returns were compiled monthly and are virtually complete, and are a useful substitute for the bills of entry in this postwar period.

MDHB/S   1946 - 1959   14 Boxes

Operational Records

This section covers the day-to-day operations of the Harbour Master's and Warehouse Manager's departments. Except for the dock registers, this section is only roughly listed and *can only be consulted by appointment*. However, the Committee papers (MDHB/COM) and the Worked-up papers (MDHB/WUP) are excellent substitutes. These are also amplified by the work of the Dockland History Project, notably in A. Johnson's "Working the Tides" and in the digests of extracts from the MDHB Archives compiled by the Merseyside Docklands History Survey. The Piermaster's House, which is part of the Maritime Museum, provides a three-dimensional perspective on the working of the port.

The Dock Registers show the date of the vessel entering a dock, its name, master's name, owner or consignees, registered tonnage, draught, where from, when berthed, date of leaving, a very brief description of the cargo (usually only one word, e.g., salt, coal, ice, very often "general" or "light"). In very few cases are passengers or emigrants mentioned. These are the definitive record of a vessel's arrival or departure from a dock; they also cover all movements *within* the dock system – for example, from a discharging berth to a loading berth or to a graving dock.

Though a valuable source, they are difficult to use – first, because they are compiled by dock, or by dock group and second, they are totally unindexed. They are also quite heavy and some need rebinding.

Studies of these records can be found in the Merseyside Docklands History Survey for the South docks, i.e. from Canning to Herculaneum. Most of the essential information on arrival, sailing dates and cargo is more easily accessible in Lloyd's List or the Customs Bill of Entry.

MDHB/OP/1   1827 - 1966   approx 520 Volumes

Other Operational Records cover the detailed day-to-day work in the docks, including tobacco and other imports at Albert Dock and grain at the Waterloo warehouses. Statistics for individual commodities are available in other sections of the MDHB collection. Some are roughly sorted, many are in need of repair. Partial interim lists are available. *They can only be consulted by appointment.*
MDHB/OP/2   c. 1900 - 1970   approx. 50 Boxes

Books of Rates and Charges for Docks and Warehouses

This gives a comprehensive picture of the variety of cargoes handled by the port over the past 150 years. It consists of annotated tables of rates, charges and warehouse rents with correspondence.
MDHB/DR   1846 - 1960   8 Boxes

Engineer's Department Records

The Engineer-in-Chief (or the Surveyor of the Docks before 1858) had the same status as the Secretary of the Board and was the highest paid officer. He (and the Solicitor to the Board) continued to occupy a higher status than the other heads of department after the establishment of the General Manager's post in 1894. The Engineer-in-Chief took overall responsibility for the design, construction and maintenance of all docks and other facilities apart from navigational marks and salvage.

The maps, plans and drawings which have been gradually acquired from 1974 have been made into a separate section (see MDHB/M/D).

Other sections which provide information on the engineer's work include the Committee papers (MDHB/COM), the Worked-Up papers (MDHB/WUP) and for works before 1859 the Early Miscellaneous papers (MDHB/D/T). The Merseyside Docklands History Survey records contain extracts from the MDHB Archives classified by subject or South Dock (i.e., from Chester Basin to Herculaneum Dock) and A.E. Jarvis and others have written extensively about the work of individual engineers and their relationship with the Board (see MDHB references).

Total Cost of Work Ledgers
This series of massive volumes illustrates the large extent of the Dock Board engineering activities. The financial breakdown is extremely detailed and almost complete for 1868-1887.
MDHB/ENG/1   1868-1887   19 Volumes

Engineer's Expenditure (slim volumes)
MDHB/ENG/2   1889 - 1964   12 Boxes

Report books, 1829-1872; Annual reports and accounts, 1837-1865; various volumes of accounts, 1848-1935; contracts book, 1822-1859; contracts 1899-1952; specifications, 1863-1901; Commonplace books (miscellaneous items including drawings, advertisements etc.), 1865-1928; miscellaneous items including photographs, 1764-1966.
MDHB/ENG/3-12   1764-1966   approx. 300 Volumes

Marine Surveyor's and Water Bailiff's Department Records

The depth of water in the Mersey and its approaches was of crucial importance. The Marine Surveyor's Department conducted regular surveys of docks, entrances, the upper estuary and Liverpool Bay and took responsibility for marking navigational hazards by buoys, three lightships, four lighthouses and a number of landmarks. It also took responsibility for removing hazards such as wrecks and published annually revised charts of the Mersey and Liverpool Bay.
Letter Books – Manuscript copies of indexed letters written from the Marine Surveyor's Office. Letters to Jesse Hartley, Dock Surveyor, occur throughout.
                    1838 - 1850   2 Volumes in 1 Box

Notice to Mariners – Printed posters announcing movement of lightships and buoys, changes in procedure, the position of wrecks and any other things of navigational importance to users.
Buoy Books – Registers of maintenance and changes, e.g., Buoy F 4/3 Red Conical - 29 August 1924. Renumbered in accordance with Notice to Mariners dated 31 July 1924.
                    1885 - 1958   3 Volumes in 2 Boxes
MDHB/M/S   1838 - 1958   7 Boxes

Maps, Plans and Drawings

This section is one of the largest and most problematic sections of the whole Archives. They are mainly derived from the Engineer's Department and include Ordnance Survey and other published maps used by or adapted for MDHB uses; charts of the estuary and docks area specially drawn; engineering and architectural drawings of docks, buildings, fittings, machinery of MDHB; docks and works with which the Chief Engineers were involved in other areas of Britain; and drawings from other ports acquired or made for comparison. Problems include the poor condition of many plans through hard usage and the inclusion of many schemes and proposals which were not carried out. To make matters worse, apparently minor pencilled additions can indicate a crucial element in the execution of a proposal. It is estimated that there are 30,000 drawings in total. Many have been microfilmed to a varying standard by the Dock Company. The Archives holds a quantity of these reels for important plans of the South Docks.

This section can only be described at the moment in a very summary manner and it is divided into sub-sections by storage location.

Sub-section A
Held in the Maritime Archives and Library at the Albert Dock Building

A large plan of the Old Dock, Salthouse Dock, and the proposed Georges Dock by Timothy Lightoller, Architect, drawn to illustrate works proposed under the Liverpool Dock Act 1761. It includes drawings of a number of types of vessel.
MDHB/M/D/1   1765   1 Roll

A large plan by W. Jessop of the Liverpool Docks in 1800.
MDHB/M/D/2   1800   1 Folder

Plans of the Docks south of Princes Dock only.
MDHB/M/D/Drawers A (Microfilms available) c.1820 - c.1970 approx 84 Drawers

Plans of most Docks, c.1830 - c.1970
MDHB/M/D/Drawers B (to be renumbered)

Rolled plans, very roughly listed, c.1850 - 1970
MDHB/M/D/Rolls

2 Boxes of commercially produced plans, showing dock development.
MDHB/M/D/Boxes 1 & 2   c.1832 - c.1910 2 Boxes

OS Maps adapted for dock company use.
MDHB/M/D/Drawers C c.1850 - 1910   c. 6 Drawers

Plans of vessels acquired by the Engineers to assess access to docks and the landing stage (list available)
MDHB/M/D/Drawers D   approx. 5 Drawers

Charts, from MDHB, Mersey Conservancy and other sources, c.1750 - c.1970.
MDHB/M/D/Drawers E   2 Drawers

Plans of Bidston Observatory, Lighthouses and light vessels, c. 1800 - c. 1950.
MDHB/M/D/Drawers F   approx. 8 Drawers

Sub-section B
Plans and Drawings held in the North Street Store
Note: the number in brackets indicates the number of drawers occupied.

Grouped by Dock: Birkenhead (Wirral) (21), Princes (15), Royal Seaforth (10), Landing Stage/Riverside Station (9), Waterloo (6), New North (5), George's and Duke's (2), Central (2), Graving (2), Gladstone (1), Huskisson (1), and Herculaneum (1).
MDHB/MD Drawers G   84 Drawers

Grouped by Technical Aspects: machinery (including cranes) (12), technical (8), bridges (5), buildings (4), coal/high level railway (3), walks (3), dock gates (2), boilers (1), canteens, etc. (1), weighbridges (1), and workshops (1).
MDHB/MD Drawers H   41 Drawers

Grouped by Subject: ARP (World War II) (3), OS Maps (3), overhead railway (3), trams (2), sewers (2), warehouse and factory acts (2), other ports (2), B and I Ferry terminal, borings, Clarence Dock Power Station, Inland Sorting Depot, ore and oil terminals, quarries, private work of Jesse Hartley, reorganisation of Dock Board, ro-ro vessels, Runcorn Bridge, telegraph station, United Molasses Depot, Regent Road, Vulcan dredger (1 drawer or less each)
MDHB/M/D/Drawers I   Total 38 drawers

There are also approximately 250 boxes of plans, yet to be documented.

Wreck Files

These relate to wrecks in and around the Mersey and its approaches. Some 235 files have survived. They vary in content, but most are quite comprehensive and include *Notices to Mariners* and newspaper cuttings, some of which give results of Board of Trade enquiries. The earliest file is that of the SS *Flamingo*, which collided with SS *Glenmor* off Canada Basin on 10 February 1881. War losses include SS *Tacoma City*, sunk in the southern part of the river by enemy action on 13 March 1941 and the steam tug *Denham* sank after hitting a mine on Wallasey Beach on 18 July 1946. The last file is that of the yacht *Deltet* which sank off New Brighton on 13 April 1950. The MDHB usually took responsibility for any salvage work and these operations are recorded in other sections, including the photograph section. The series is unfortunately incomplete.
MDHB/WR/1-235   1881-1950   26 Boxes

Vessels of MDHB

The MDHB owned a large number of service vessels including dredgers, hopper barges, pilot boats, salvage and buoying vessels, survey launches, floating cranes, tugs and barges. References to these craft can be found throughout the MDHB including the committee papers (MDHB/COM), the Worked-Up papers (MDHB/WUP), the maps, plans and drawings (MDHB/M/D), newscuttings (MDHB/N/C) photographs (MDHB/PHO) and pilotage service (MDHB/PIL). The museum collections also include models of MDHB vessels, the gig from the Board's tender, *Galate* (1906), and the pilot vessel *Edmund Gardner* (1953). The *Salvor* (1947) and the *Vigilant* (1953) were employed on surveying, buoy maintenance and salvage. The museum also holds a photographic and film record of the steamer *Vigilant's* last working days in 1979 as well as the furnishings of her master's cabin.
Tender *Salvor* Log books 1947-1976
Tender *Vigilant* Log books, etc. 1953-1976; work books 1960-1974
memoranda books, 1949-1962; misc. papers 1950-1977
MDHB/V   1947 - 1977   7 Boxes

Staff and Wages Records

The MDHB was a major employer of all kinds of labour in the port and this section includes some detailed records of employees. They include Register of officers including names and duties of all officers on salary, date of appointment, salaries, promotions, superannuations, etc. (indexed), 1846-1950; list of weekly servants, general Vol. 1 (indexed), c. 1880-1940; accident report books (all departments), 1880-1931; registers of accidents (factory and workshop acts, etc.), 1903-1933; register of dangerous occurrences (factory and workshop notice of accidents act, 1906), 1907-1946; accident reports pursuant to National (Industrial Injuries) Act 1946, 1947-1948 (1 volume); various personnel department papers; rates of wages register, 1936-1985; statistical analysis of manpower by trade, 1967-1971; conditions of employment, 1946; and sick pay schemes, 1945.
MDHB/SW   1846-1985   22 Boxes

Uniform of Employees

Many operational employees such as piermasters, dockgate men and seamen wore the Board's uniform. These files include specimens of buttons and badges, sketches of cuffs, etc., and are supplemented by a series of complete uniforms in the Maritime History department.
MDHB/U   1907 - 1947   2 Boxes

New Head Offices at Pier Head

The papers relating to the Mersey Dock and Harbour Board's 1908 office building comprise files of architects' tenders, contracts and bills of quantities, correspondence about estimates, payments, departmental requirements with manufacturers of materials; also four small interior plans and an original photograph of the Dock Offices from the River Mersey, 1907. Plans of the building can be found in the plans section.

MDHB/DO   1899 - 1916   4 Boxes

National Dock Labour Board

This collection consists of the Mersey Dock and Harbour Board's own files on dock labour issues and its relations with the National Dock Labour Board: annual reports, accounts, financial and general papers; minutes of meetings; papers re: dock strikes; proposed revision of the Dock Labour Scheme; specialist labour and labour and retirement of dock workers. No names of dock workers are given.

MDHB/NDLB   1943-1960   9 Boxes

Port Defence

These papers show the concern of the Dock Board for the defence of the port. Earlier defence arrangements for the Mersey can be found in the Worked Up papers (MDHB/WUP) and the maps, plans and drawings (MDHB/M/D). Accommodation for men at Ormeshead, Port Lynas and Formby Lightship in the event of war, a proposed guardship in the River, marking of "friendly" channels through minefields by night, protection of dock gates, tugs for examination service, Notices to Pilots etc.

MDHB/PD   1898 - 1950   2 Boxes

Port Emergency Committee

In 1936 the Ministry of Transport set up a Port and Transit Committee in London, an off-shoot of the Committee of Imperial Defence, to prepare emergency schemes under which ports could operate under war conditions. Port Emergency Committees were established in the major ports. The prewar functions of the Committee were to prepare a scheme for making the best use of the facilities of the ports including rapid clearance of the quays. The Liverpool Port Emergency Committee consisted of a member of the MDHB, its General Manager and Secretary, and representatives of coastwise and overseas shipping, canals, railways, road haulage and general trading interests. On 6 January 1945 the committee became known as the Area Liaison Committee.

These documents give a clear insight into the work of the committee and the efforts of the port from the prewar period to its recovery after the war.

Volumes of minute books (5) 1942-1947; files of memoranda and correspondence covering P.E.C. before the war; warehousing, storage, quay and cargo files include military fire watching, segregation and storage of foodstuffs in public warehouses; disposal of unexploded bombs; insurance against war risk and the use of ships for storage purposes; records re: land transport; the employment of British and U.S. military labour and civil defence; role of Merchant seamen in the allied invasion of the continent; pilferage; blitz; N.W. Regional Port Directors.

MDHB/PEC/1/1-13/4   1936-1955   15 Boxes

Port Labour Committee

This series of letter books deals mainly with the exemption of dock workers from military service during World War I.

MDHB/PLC   1915 - 1919   5 Boxes

Printed Material

This consists of four sub-sections: Parliamentary acts, bills and enquiries; pamphlets from the Secretary's office; by-laws and regulations; and printed bound volumes of lawsuits.

Parliamentary Acts, Bills & Enquiries

This series covers all the wide variety of Parliamentary issues which the Dock Company and its antecedents initiated or in which it had an interest. It is not completely listed but among the important items are the Liverpool Dock Acts of 1709 (original black letter imprint) 1716, 1737, 1761, 1784, 1799. These are all bound with the Act of 1811. Other business is covered from 1840 to 1919 and this includes private bills and wider matters such as parliamentary reports on national issues, for example, the report on Local Charges on Shipping of 1856. After 1919 there is a gap until 1954 and the series ends with the MDHB (Seaforth Works) Bill enquiry of 1966.

MDHB/P/1   1709 - 1966   c. 30 Boxes

Pamphlets

This miscellaneous section from the office of the MDHB's Secretary, is arranged under twenty-one artificial headings as follows:-

1.   Mersey Conservancy Commission Reports, 1842-1927

2.   Mersey Docks and Estuary, 1891-1934
3.   Dredging Operations (mainly on Mersey), 1893-1906
4.   Chairman's Annual Address, Mersey Docks and Harbour Board, 1902-1908
5.   Trade of the Port of Liverpool, 1903-1946
6.   Reconstructions, extensions and foundations of Docks generally, 1905-1934
7.   Liverpool Dock Labour Inquiry, 1912-1914
8.   Industry and Casual Labour, 1925-1932
9.   Liverpool Steamship Owners Association, 1924-1931
10. Liverpool Chamber of Commerce (Special Committee Reports), 1879-1880
11. International Conference on Safety at Sea, 1914-1929
12. Railway Administration, 1881-1915
13. Transport, Local and National, 1833-1965
14. The Manchester Ship Canal, 1883-1886
15. Local Authority Reports, 1843-1936
16. Police Force, 1893-1895
17. Papers read to the Liverpool Engineering Society, 1886-1917
18. Presidential Addresses, Institution of Civil Engineers, 1907-1919
19. Reports of Royal Commissions, 1923-1937
20. Reports on general Parliamentary matters, 1928-1939
21. Miscellaneous, 1891-1948

Category 1 contains reports of the government-appointed body for ensuring that the Mersey is in a navigable condition. Categories 7 and 8 are highly relevant to the question of casual labour on the docks and include the studies in the aftermath of the 1911 strike. Category 10 contains material on the question of whether the Port of Liverpool was overcharging its customers. Category 11 contains material sparked off by the sinking of the *Titanic* in 1912. Category 15 contains the early report on the sanitary conditions in the Birkenhead dock area.
MDHB/P/2   1842 - 1965   6 Boxes

By-Laws and Regulations

Four volumes containing copies of the by-laws and regulations from 1866 to 1875. Additions up to 1888 have been added. Also included are lists of dock charges, a table of the sizes of docks being used in 1888, copies of letters written to shipowners warning them not to tip employees and a list of police beats and stations. The third volume includes instructions for the use of foghorns and regulations for the management of the lifeboat service, and the fourth is a bound compilation of rules, conditions, printed reports and Parliamentary Acts.
MDHB/P/3   1858 - 1965   2 Boxes

Printed Bound Volumes of Lawsuits, Including Appeals, Arbitrations, etc.

Bound volumes of MDHB lawsuits and arbitrations between 1827 and 1904, including arbitrations between railway companies and MDHB, MDHB v. Corporation of Liverpool, MDHB v. Co-operative Wholesale Society Limited, MDHB v. Manchester Ship Canal, and other lawsuits in the issue of which MDHB had an interest.

Other particularly interesting cases are:-

The King v. S Grimshaw and others, Lancashire Summer Assizes, 1827. (This relates to the diversion of water from the Mersey at Woolston, upriver from Warrington, which affected the navigation of the river by silting. A large number of flatmen and fishermen were cross-examined.)

Liverpool Corn Trade Association v. London and North Western Railway, 1890-1892.

W.H. Turner and owners of *Zeta* v. MDHB, Appeal, House of Lords, 1892.

Owners of No. 7 Steam Sand Pump Dredger and owners of SS *Greta Holme* Appeal, House of Lords, 1896.

Owners of SS *Mediana* v. owners, masters and crew of Lightship *Comet*, Appeal, House of Lords, 1898.

SS Fulda, Norddeutscher Lloyd v. MDHB and Clover Clayton & Co. 1899.

Arbitration regarding purchase price of site of George's Dock by Liverpool Corporation, 1899.

Arbitration regarding Duke's Dock, Liverpool, between MDHB and Manchester Ship Canal, 1900.

MDHB/P/4   1827 - 1904   7 Boxes

Public Relations

This comprises two sections: yearbooks and dock openings and royal visits. The Board's newspaper *Port News* and annual handbooks/guides to shipping are to be found in the library section (16).

Yearbooks

These contain basic facts about the Board's administration, names of members and key officers, with folding plans of the dock estate, dates of board and committee meetings, and many useful dimensions and dates of docks and shipping lines' use of specific docks. There are also runs of association copies.
MDHB/PR/1   1882 - 1970   4 Boxes

Dock Openings and Royal Visits

These programmes and pamphlets mark new developments, royal visits, etc. going back to 1911 and including the opening of Gladstone Dock in 1927 and the visit by King George V. Other examples are found in the Worked Up papers (MDHB/WUP) and accounts can also be found in the newscuttings section (MDHB/N/C & NC/L)
MDHB/PR/2   1911 - 1984   5 Boxes

Newscuttings

There is an unclassified series in order of date, 1890-1907. Most bound news-cuttings are by subject and range from 1875 to 1971. The unbound files range from 1878 to 1971. It is not clear why there were two series, but they may have been kept by different offices. The clerks were meticulous in assembling them and the coverage is both local and national. Both bound, except for the unclassified volumes, and unbound are also topically indexed. The following is a selection of the topics covered.

Bound Volumes

Shipping Companies

Blue Funnel Line (Alfred Holt & Co.)	1966-1971
Canadian Pacific Steamship Company Ltd. and Canadian	
Pacific Railway Company Ltd.	1963-1971
Cunard and White Star Line	1927-1971
Elder Dempster Lines Ltd.	1964-1971
Isle of Man Steam Packet Company and North Wales	1964-1971
Pacific Steam Navigation Company Ltd.	1964-1971

The Port of Liverpool and Individual Docks

British Transport Docks Board: General Docks	1963-1971
Customs of the Port	1963-1971

Director General of Mersey Docks and Harbour Board	1952-1971
Dock Improvements	1924-1971
Docking and Discharging: Quick Turn-Around	1963-1971
Dock Offences, Thefts, Robberies etc.	1929-1966
Dock Police	1905-1971
Dock Rates and Town Dues	1963-1971
Dock Strikes	1962-1971
Garston Docks	1964-1969
Graving Docks	1883-1946
	1952-1971
Opening of Langton River Entrance by HM Queen - Dec 1962	1962
Port Charges	1932-1971
The Port of Liverpool and Merseyside Social Events	1930-1971
Port Traffic Returns, Vessels Using the Port	1963-1969
(See also "other subjects")	

Canal and Rivers

Birkenhead Ship Canal (never constructed)	1884-1889
Birmingham – Canals Running Through Between the Mersey,	
Severn and Humber	1885-1941
Canals and Inland Waterways	1964-1971
Industrial Rivers of the United Kingdom	1889
Panama Canal	1914-1968
Pollution of Rivers and Sewage Schemes	1928-1971
Railway and Canal Traffic	1933-1971
River Clyde	1937-1971
River Dee Improvements	1963-1971
River Tees: Middlesbrough, Hartlepool	1901-1971
River Tyne Commissioners	1928-1971
River Wear, Sunderland	1902-1971
Suez Canal	1927-1969

Royal Visits

Coronation of George V – 1911 and Jubilee – 1935	1911,1935
Coronation of King Edward VII	1902
Investiture of Prince of Wales	1911
King Edward VIII, Abdication, Coronation of King George VI	
and Coronation of Queen Elizabeth	1936-1958
The King's Visit	1917
Royal Visits to Birkenhead, Port Sunlight and Wallasey	1913-1959
Visits of Royalty and Other Distinguished Persons to Liverpool	1938-1971

Trades

Cattle Trade Accommodation	1933-1971
Coal Trade	1935-1971
Cotton	1926-1971
Fruit Trade	1964-1971
Municipal Trading	1906-1912
Salt Trade	1886-1918
Timber Trade	1953-1971
Tobacco Trade	1963-1970
Trade (Shipping)	1933-1971
The Wool Trade	1964-1971

Other Ports

Australia and New Zealand	1922-1969
Belfast and the Port of North Ireland	1941-1971
Berehaven Harbour and Proposed Atlantic Mail Line	1901
Boston and Philadelphia	1913-1927
Bristol and Avonmouth	1925-1971
Canadian Harbours and Saint Lawrence Seaway	1913-1971
Cardiff, Newport and the South Wales Port	1952-1971
European Ports: Antwerp, Rotterdam, Amsterdam, Hamburg	1929-1971
Greenock Harbour Trust	1913-1970
Hull, Grimsby and Immingham	1927-1971
Irish Ports	1963-1971
Mails and Fishguard	1963-1971
Milford Haven	1963-1971
Millwall Dock Company	1911-1971
Miscellaneous Harbours	1899-1912
Plymouth	1924-1971
Port of London	1915-1971
Port of Manchester and Manchester Ship Canal Company	1928-1971
Port of New York and American Seaports	1937-1971
Port of Preston and the River Ribble	1919-1971
Port of Southampton	1905-1970
Ports on the River Forth, Leith and Grangemouth	1923-1971
Royal Commission on the Port of London, Evidence	1888-1971
Runcorn and the Upper Mersey Navigation	1900-1901
Surrey Commercial Dock Company	1963-1971
Swansea	1887-1909

Other Subjects

Accidents	1891-1971
Aerial Undertakings	1969
Board of Trade Eyesight Tests	1909-1914
British Association Meetings	1907-1960
Cargo Handling, Container Traffic and Crane Accommodation	1962-1971
Chamber of Shipping and Liverpool Steamship Owners Assn.	1935-1971
Channel Tunnel	1963-1971
Claims Against the Board	1882-1937
Coastal Erosion: Foreshore Land, Otterspool etc.	1965-1970
Cold Storage	1913-1960
Congestion of Traffic	1919-1971
Corn Warehouses	1933-1971
Diesel Motorships	1912-1957
Electric Light and Power	1963-1970
Employees Liability Act: Workmen Compensation Act	1913-1958
Explosives	1911-1970
Fires and Fire Prevention	1941-1971
Hopper Barges and Dredgers	1940-1966
Hovercraft and Hydrofoil	1963-1971
Inland Navigation	1899-1930
Inquiry into Shipping	1967-1971
International Press Cuttings	1946-1952
Lancashire Plateway	1882-1915
Law Reports and Legal Precedents in Mercantile Law	1876-1938
Lighthouses and Lightvessels	1963-1971
Lighting and the Approaches to the Port, Fog Horns etc.	1930-1970
Liverpool Chamber of Commerce	1934-1971
Liverpool Landing Stage	1908-1937
Liverpool Miscellany	1875-1915
Liverpool Overhead Railway Company	1877-1960
Loss of the *Titanic*, April 1912	1913-1914
Lusitania: Sunk May 7, 1915	1915
Manchester Chamber of Commerce	1902-1920
Mersey Bar and Dredging	1884-1931
Mersey Conservancy and the Silting of Channels	1963-1971
Mersey Ferries	1924-1971
Mersey Tunnel	1928-1971
Mr. John Rankin and Party Continental Cruise	1914
Nuclear Power: Installations and Vessels	1958-1970
Oil Discharging Facilities in Liverpool Bay	1969
Oil in Navigable Waters	1963-1971

Petrol and Oil, Liquid Gases, Pipelines, Tankers, Tranmere Oil Stages	1933-1971
Pier Head, Dock Offices and Customs House: Improvements	1913-1964
Pilotage	1934-1971
The Pluckington Bank	1880-1934
Quarantine Regulations	1910-1966
Riverside Station	1912-1960
Royal Commission Enquiry into the Working of the Railway Conciliation Scheme	1911-1959
Salvage: Liverpool and Glasgow Salvage Association	1964-1970
The Seaforth Project: Container Terminal	1964-1971
Shipbuilding	1934-1971
Shipping Combines	1902-1960
Shipping Subsidies	1910-1968
Strikes and Labour	1941-1971
Telegraphic communications Wireless Telegraphy and Radar	1932-1971
Trade Salvage	1944-1946
Trans Atlantic Competition	1914-1935
Transfer of White Star Passenger Steamers from Liverpool to Southampton	1907-1909
Vessels Anchoring in the Track of Ferry Boats	1878-1911
War	1940-1966
Wrecks	1931-1970
MDHB/NC 237 Boxes	

Unbound Volumes

Shipping Companies

Allan Bros (UK) Ltd.	1910
Anchor Line (Henderson Bros)	1901
Beaver Line, transfer to CDR	1903
Canadian Pacific Railway & Steamship Companies	1903-1963
City of Dublin in Steam Packet	1899-1915
Elder Dempster & Co.	1899-1967
F. Leyland & Co.	1892-1913
Harrison, T. & J.	1916
Henderson Bros. Ltd.	1899-1911
Isle of Man Steam Packet Co.	1903-1963
Orient SS Co.	1905
Pacific SN Co.	1905-1963
Railway Companies' Steamers	1888-1935
Steam Fishing and Cold Storage Company	1897-1900

White Star Line   1898-1930

Docks

Alfred Dock Inner and Outer Entrances Estimates	1926
Alfred Dock Gates Burst Open	1920
British Transport Commission Docks	1962-1963
Clarence Dock Site Purchased by Corporation	1928-1963
Dead House, Princes Dock	1888
Detention of Cargo at Docks and Quays	1889
Dukes Dock Property – Manchester Ship Canal	1899-1900
Garston Dock	1878-1963
George's Dock Bridge	1886-1897
Huskisson Dock	1966
Naming of Docks	1888
North Dockyard Closing at Dundas Street	1902
Public Houses on Dock Estate	1892
Robberies – Docks and Quays	1893-1935
State Aided Docks	1906

Other Subjects

A

Accidents	1892-1937
Accommodation for Coal Shipments, Birkenhead	1888-1906
for the Grain Trade, Southend	
Aeroplanes etc. from Speke Airport (3 vols.)	1928-1955
	1955-1960
American Merchant Marine	1905
American Visitors and Liverpool	1903
Appropriation of Berths Foreign Trade part 1	1887-1914
Armed Merchant Cruises	1913-1917
Armed Merchant Men	1940

B

Bank of Liverpool	1903-1928
Berth Accommodation, Manchester and Liverpool Transport	
Company	1902-1904
Boards	1883-1911
Boyle, Sir Courtenay, death of	1901
Bridgewater Companies Improvement of Mersey and Irwell	1884-1906

British Empire Exhibition   1921-1951
British Ports   1907

C

Canals   1889-1960
Channel Tunnel   1913-1963
Collard V Houston
Collision at Sea   1878
Crimping   1903-1909
Customs House, Liverpool   1899
Customs of the Port   1891-1962

D

Decline of the Trade of the Port   1879-1906
Depression of Trade at Bootle   1901-
Dogs, Importation of   1897-1918

E

Emigration   1897-1914
European War   1914
Exhibition   1916-1937

F

Foreign   1906-1930
Fruit: Dues of Trade   1893-1963

G

George V HM Death of   1936
George VI HM death of   1952
German Prisoners of War – Employment   1916-1918
Great Eastern   1886-1960

H

Haresford, SS Explosion on...   1966
Hill, Sir John Grey, death of   1914-
Historical Liverpool Steamship Companies   1889
Holzapfel, A.G.   1916

Hydraulic Power Co., Liverpool	1889

I

Incendiarism, Riots etc.	1920-1955
Indian Famine Board	1897-1901
Inquiry into Shipping	1967-1970
International Maritime Committee	1898-1927
International Inland Navigation Congress	1890-1923
International Shipping Conference	1924-1935
Irish Channel Tunnel, Proposed	1899-1907

L

Laird Brothers	1903-1910
Leeds and Liverpool Improvements	1889-1960
Lever Brothers	1924-1960
Liverpool:Is Liverpool a Decaying City?	1904-1929
Developments of Industries	
Dock Ratepayers' Association	1883
In the Great War	1919-1920
Steamship Owners' Association	1898-1993
	1934-1953
Warehousing Company	1895-1959

M

Ministry of Shipping	1939-1941

O

Oil Fuel	1910, 1922
Old Liverpool	1922-1924
Onita, PS MC V MD MB	1901

P

Port Sanitary Authority	1893-1963
	1964-1971
Prevention of Corruption Bill	1903-1907
Proposed Irish Channel Tunnel	1899-1907

Q

Queen Victoria Memorial	1901

R

Riverside Cold Storage Company	1898-1911
Royal Naval Reserve	

S

Sailing, Shipowners, International Union of	1903-1937
Sea Fisheries Regulations Act	1889-1912
Ship Canal Between Southampton and London	1901-1907
Shipping Crisis	1890
Shipping Disasters (not wrecks)	1890-1931
Shipping Federation	1890
Shipping, Ministry of	1939-1941
Shipping Regulations and Foreign Ships	1890
Shipowners' Association, Liverpool	1898-1933
	1934
South Lancashire and Cheshire Coal Association	1889
South Wales Coal Mining Dispute	1934
Sugar Bounties	1899-1907

T

Thetis HM Submarine	1939-1958
Timber Trade	1885-1955
	1956-1963
Tin Plate Trade	1897
Tobacco Trade	1891-1959
Toll on Ferry Goods Traffic and Birkenhead Corporation Bill	1886-1891
Tonnage Dues Overseas on Partially Discharging and Loading in the Port	1886-1889
Training Ships	1896-1962
Transfer of Bonds etc Forged Transfer Acts	1892-1916
Transport Advisory Council	1934-1938
Truck Acts 1846	1891-1913

U

University, Liverpool	1960-1963
US Shipping Bill	1920-1922

V

Vanished and Vanishing Institutions	1910

W

Warehouse Disaster, Liverpool	1919
Wild Bird Protection Act, Destruction of Sea Birds	
Wool Trade	1898-1916
MDHB/NC/L	40 Boxes

Photographs

The Board used photographs to record the construction of docks, cargo handling, accidents and visual evidence for court cases probably from its inception. The earliest surviving photographs are a montage of the Pier Head and the landing stages of about 1860 (undergoing conservation at present). The opening of Birkenhead docks in 1866 is another early view. The company also possessed a number of albums containing dock building and dock work from about 1870 to 1900 in the early 1970s which seem to have disappeared. But many of the images were copied by the Liverpool Museum photographer and the copy negatives are held by the NMGM central services photography department with a list held in the Maritime Archives. This collection is divided into the main collection (MDHB/PHO/1) and other accumulations (MDHB/PHO/2).

Main Collection

This consists of some 276 prints and about 3000 glass negatives from about 1906 to 1939. The prints are listed and indexed. The negatives are listed but the lists need more research. Copy prints are being produced at the moment. They provide a wide coverage of work in the port including cargo handling, such as lifting railway locomotives, passenger liners at the landing stage, and road and railway traffic on the dock estate. The negatives contain copies of older views of docks. Many of the more spectacular pictures were used in the Board's publications and appear to be the work of the Board's own photographer.

Other Photographic Accumulations

Most of these photographs originated in the Engineer's department and they include some of the earliest photographs. The majority are mounted. Some are extremely fragile. Subjects include cranes, c.1860 - c.1900 (17, including very early examples from West Float, Birkenhead, c.1860; movable coaling cranes; locally manufactured cranes from the works of James Taylor & Co., Birkenhead; Dunlop, Bell and Co., and John H. Wilson and Co. Ltd., both of Liverpool. Many of these photographs are not in Mersey Dock estate settings); coaling plant and elevated railway, Bramley Moore and Wellington Docks, c. 1910 (14); naming of Alfred Dock and fifty foot lock, Birkenhead, by Duke of Edinburgh, 1866 (2); salvage of sailing vessel *J.C. Boynton*, whose master, in an effort to exit Prince's half-tide dock on a swiftly ebbing tide, stranded the vessel on the sill, 23 August 1871 (6); model of proposed overhead railway 1884 (4); overhead railway track, 1890; Riverside Railway Station 1895 (2); railway lines, Prince's Dock, c. 1900 (3 identical); Birkenhead Dock Entrance, c. 1920; dock and building construction, including Robinson's subaqueous rock drilling operations c. 1890-1900 (12); dock scenes, in dredgers; and a small album of four photographs advertising Henrebiques Patent Constructions in Ferro concrete with album of photographs of crushing test results, 1900.

Commercial Photograph Album
Welsh and Scott, Engineers, Manchester, c. 1876 (with five enclosures)

Commercial Brochures
Clark and Standfield's Double Power Floating Dock, 1878
Clark and Standfield's Depositing Dock (with photograph of *SS Odessa* at
          Nicolaieff, 1878)
Pumping Stations, stationary engines, etc. c. 1880-1920

Further large albums relate to construction of Alexandra and Waterloo docks, opened September 1881; progress of work on Brunswick river entrance, 1901-1902; official photographs of bomb damage to the docks 1 & 2 September 1940; official photographs at Huskisson No. 2 Branch dock in September 1943, showing the remains of *SS Malakand*; and views of lighting systems to docks, roadways, transit sheds, graving docks and shed interiors dated 24 October 1952, (a number of loose photographs of similar views dated May 1954 complement this album), loose photographs: *Queen Elizabeth* photographed in wartime colours as a troopship on 5 April 1945 and an aerial view of South docks from Prince's dock on 9 August 1947.
MDHB/PHO   c.1860 - 1954   4 Boxes

Miscellaneous Volumes

1. **Liverpool Docks – Extracts from Acts of Parliament and Financial Returns**: A valuable source of secondary material 1709-1855.

2. **Manchester, Bolton and Bury Canal Navigation and Railroad 1832-1835**: A private commission of Jesse Hartley, Surveyor and Engineer to the Dock Trust.

3. **Charitable Fund Casebook 1833-1851**: The casebook illustrates that while no sick or compensation schemes were in operation there were funds available for the "deserving poor." Applicants for relief ranged from a sick widow living alone in a cellar kitchen, to a whole family rendered destitute by the loss of the breadwinner. The wife of a deceased former dock employee was granted the sum of £4 in order to purchase a mangle, with which to support herself and her four children. The fund was also used to reward those attempting to rescue the drowning. Those rescued were taken to "receiving houses." Rewards did not depend upon successful rescue and both the "house" and the rescuer were rewarded. The funds came from fines levied against persons convicted of stealing from the docks.

3a. **Charitable Fund Annual Account Book 1862-1929**

4. **Liverpool Dock Police Books (2 volumes) 1835-1836**: A record of persons suspected of committing offences on the docks.

5. **Liverpool Dock Gateman's Friendly Burial Society Minute Book**: Annual General Meeting minutes 1861-1954.

6. **Register of Licensed Riggers 1879-1892**: Index of names and addresses of those persons licensed by MDHB to move vessels about the docks and river. Representation was made by the Shipowners' Association and the Liverpool Steamship Owners' Association that the practice of licensing riggers be abolished, giving the owners freedom to employ and the riggers freedom to tender for work and, since the Liverpool Riggers' Association was in agreement, the system was abolished from 1 November 1892.

7. **Memorial and Obituary Book** of Alfred Chandler, MDHB General Manager for forty-two years, died 1 March 1923.

8. **Visitor's Book, British Empire Exhibition 1924**

9.   **Scrap Book**: Containing invitation cards to various functions, e.g., the opening of the new Liverpool Royal Infirmary by HRH Duke of Clarence and Avondale on 29 October 1890. Many are addressed in person to Miles K. Burton, Secretary to MDHB. The cards are most attractive, with representations of buildings, ships, etc., in colour, 1881-1897.

MDHB/MV   1709 - 1929   3 Boxes and 2 loose volumes

Early Miscellaneous Papers

This section contains a wealth of material mainly from about 1790 to 1890, except for sections 5 and 8. It was collected by the Assistant Secretary's office. Lists for the majority of this section are only available in very rough draft form, and *access is by appointment only*.

1.   Committee Reports etc. re: improvements and Dock extensions c.1839-44; Reports re: position of gunpowder magazines 1881-1890.

2.   Committee Reports, Notes and Evidence re: Provision of New Docks and piers, Liverpool Docks Bill etc. Includes Opinion of John Rennie Engineer, re: need for extra dock accommodation.

3.   Parliamentary Statements, Correspondence, Accounts and Petitions re: Dock Bills and Dock Acts.

4.   Parliamentary Papers re: Docks Bill 1811 including Minutes of Meetings and Correspondence from the East India Company, Mediterranean & Levant Association, British North American Association and Liverpool Shipowners Association etc; Details of Dock Estate revenue etc.

5.   Papers re: Pilotage Committee, Pilotage Annuity Fund, Gatekeepers, Customs etc. 1837-1971.

6.   Reports and Minutes of Evidence etc., re: Limits of the Port of Liverpool and Town Dues etc. Includes list of Acts of Parliament re: Liverpool, by L.P. Stubbs 1863; Book on *Corporate Tradition and National Rights* by Harriet Martineau, c. 1857.

7.   Reports and Proceedings re: abolition of Town Dues. Includes Report of Proceedings of the Association of Merchants of Liverpool 1835.

8.   Legal Department papers re: Birkenhead Docks; Includes receipts for work completed, Statements of Accounts 1847-52; Notes on Pilotage by J.T. Danson 1871, Proceedings in House of Lords, MDHB v Pilots re: pilotage rates 1890, Abstracts of Returns for U.K. Pilotage 1932-37; Correspondence re: wrecks in Garston Channel 1919-1940 etc.

9.   Minutes of Dock Committee Proceedings 1766-1839; Resolutions, Statements, Reports and Proceedings of Special and Common Council etc. 1790-1839; Correspondence with Jesse Hartley re: stages at various Docks 1840; Correspondence to Dock Committee 1839-44; Proceedings, Evidence and Report of the Special Sub-Committee on Dock Extension 1839-1844; Correspondence re: the establishment of a Dock Police Force 1809-1836; Account of Dock penalties received by the Dock Committee 1813-1815.

10.   Memorandums, Notes, Letters etc. re: legal cases eg. Birkenhead Dock Co. v Sanderson, Liverpool Dock Co. v. Gladstone 1806-64; General Administration, Staff and Dock Rate collection etc. 1811-48; Civil Service Commission Report 1875; Papers re: Bill to extend Dock Committee Powers, and re: Dock Police 1809-36; Dock Charitable Fund and penalties for misdemeanours under Dock Act 1811-1814.

11.   Minutes of Dock Committee Meetings, estimates etc. re: expenses for Liverpool Dock improvements. Includes Charles Eyes' estimate for erecting Wet Docks and a basin, 1785; Letter from Mark Isambard Brunel re: footbridge over Old Dock Entrance, 1822; Correspondence re: Dock improvement plans of M Gage, 1822-1842; Opinion of Thomas Telford, correspondence etc. re: New Graving Dock, 1821-1822.

12.   Legal cases, copies of Acts, etc., re: development of Liverpool Docks. Includes Case for building additional docks and lighthouses, payment of light duties c.1800; Case for payment of same duties by passenger vessels to Ireland, c. 1820; Copy of Proceedings of Committee of Dock Trustees and Corporation on Dock Investigation 1823. Particulars of Leases and Tenancies at Dukes Dock 1899.

13.   Correspondence re: Birkenhead Docks transfer to Liverpool Docks
        Trustees 1844-1848; Plans of property belonging to Birkenhead Dock
        Co. and proposed warehouses, 1844; Bonds & Sureties payable to the
        Dock Trustees 1840-1878; Apprenticeship Indentures, Memos, Corre-
        spondence etc. 1856-1878; Guarantee Agreements, Insurance Policies,
        etc., 1870-1881.

14.   Papers and Correspondence, etc., re: materials for Dock improvements
        1790-1800; Construction of Menai Bridge 1783-1785; Height of Tides
        at Dock gates 1794-1800; Petitions; Liverpool Streets Bill; Runcorn
        Bridge.

15.   Papers and Correspondence re: telegraph stations; Point of Ayr Light-
        house; Floating Lightships, Formby and Magazines Lifeboats,
        Hurricane damage (1839); Explosives Act, etc.

16.   Papers and Correspondence re: Purchase of land from Willis Earle
        1792-1801; Dock By-laws (1811-14); Cost Estimates for land (1792-
        1800); Lt. Evans' Survey of Coast (1812); Landing Stage at Pier Head
        (1845); Galvanised Iron for Dock improvements; Pilotage 1868-1932;
        Birkenhead Docks Bill 1844; tonnage Reports 1852; Harrington Docks
        1848-58; Minutes of Meetings re: Leeds-Liverpool Canal 1844.

17.   Papers re: Dock Duties; Purchase of Customs House; Dock Trustees
        Accounts; Liverpool Dock Debts; Dock Improvements; Dock Appoint-
        ments and Salaries; Proposed Works; Correspondence re: miscellaneous
        matters, 1765-1868.

18.   Correspondence, reports, etc., re: Birkenhead, Wallasey Embankment,
        1791-1860.

19.   Correspondence, papers, etc., re: warehouses including Apprenticeship
        indentures for warehouse clerks, 1859-1889; Bond of J.R. Davies,
        master of Salthouse Dock, 1811; Certificates, etc., of storage of cargo
        in Stanley Dock warehouses, 1858.

20.   Correspondence re: floating light vessel. Includes details of a Dublin
        light vessel 1813; purchase of Point of Air Lighthouse, 1813; estimates
        for maintaining a floating light, rates of income, etc.; Applications for
        situation of Master of the Floating Light, 1813-1824.

MDHB/DT   1752-1971   21 Boxes

Liverpool Pilotage Service

The first Liverpool Pilotage Act was passed 1766, although pilots operated before that date. The Act regulated the operation of the service and established a Pilotage Committee to oversee the working of the service including the issue of licences. Later local pilotage acts of 1797 and 1824 as well as nationwide legislation such as the Merchant Shipping Act of 1854 changed the service's operations in detail only. Responsibility for supervising and administering the service was transferred in 1858 to the MDHB, which set up its own Pilotage Committee. In 1883 the sailing pilot schooners, which had been hitherto privately owned, were transferred to the Board's ownership; but pilots remained self-employed until 1988. A new pilotage office was opened at Canning Pier Head in 1883 and this is now part of the Museum of Liverpool Life. The first steam pilot boat, *David Henderson*, was introduced in 1896 and in 1981 the service changed from the large pilot vessels to fast launches. The last large vessel, the diesel-electric *Edmund Gardner* of 1953, was acquired by the museum and is on display in the Ships and Quaysides section. The museum also owns six models of pilot boats and the official records are supplemented by the personal collection and reminiscences of the late Norman Morrison, the photographs of Barry Youd and the papers of the late J.S. Rees, the historian of the service, in the Archives of the Liverpool Nautical Research Society.

Pilotage Committee Minute Books, 1779-1859
Commissioners of Pilotage Oath Book, 1766-1857 (one volume)
Letter Book, 1854-1859 Letter & Memorandum Books (to Secretary of MDHB)
        (broken series) 1885-1887, 1908-1941.
Pilots' Character Books, 1788-1974
Other Registers, 1814-1955
Claims and Licences, 1824-1856
Registers of Masters and Rates holding Pilots' Certificates 1860-1972
Records of Candidates, 1878-1972
Byelaws, notices to pilots, office order books, 1797-1966
Newscuttings Books 1868-1971
List of vessels piloted, 1937-1968
Pilotage Annuity Fund Actuarial Reports, 1898-1949
Reports on Collisions, 1949-1961
Parliamentary Papers, inc. Acts and Bills, 1766-1949
Western Pilotage Station Board of Trade Enquiry, 1934
Log Book of No. 12 pilot boat, 1864-1868 (in Miscellaneous volumes subsec-
        tion below)
Log Books of recent pilot vessels, c.1940-1980, inc. *Edmund Gardner*
Misc. papers, 1839-1945
Misc. volumes, 1833-1965

Liverpool Pilots Mutual Benefit Society, accounts, etc. 1848-1956
MDHB/PIL   1766-1980   96 Boxes

References

General

Hyde, F.E. *Liverpool and the Mersey*. Newton Abbot, 1971. Getting dated in places, but still the best general book on Liverpool. **N.B. Useful tables of figures in appendices**.

Jackson, G. *The History and Archaeology of Ports*. Tadworth, 1983. By far the best overall coverage of British ports.

Jarvis, A. *Docks of the Mersey*. Shepperton, 1988. An outline history.

Jarvis, A. and Carron, K. *Give a Dock a Good Name?* Liverpool, 1992. A brief "biography" of each of the docks of Liverpool and Birkenhead.

Parkinson, C.N. *The Rise of the Port of Liverpool*. Liverpool, 1952. Useful on the pre-dock period.

Docks, Dock Engineers and Dock Construction

Clarke, M. "Thomas Steers." In Jarvis and Rees (eds.), *Dock Engineers and Dock Engineering*.

Cunningham, B. *Dock Engineering*. London, 1910.

Cunningham, B. *Harbour Engineering*. London, 1918.

Jarvis, A. *Liverpool Central Docks, 1799-1905*. Stroud, 1991.

Jarvis, A. "The Role of the Liverpool Dock Engineers in the Nineteenth Century." in A. Jarvis and P. Rees (eds.), *Dock Engineers and Dock Engineering*. Liverpool, 1993.

Jarvis, A. "G.F. Lyster and the Role of the Dock Engineer, 1861-97." *Mariner's Mirror*, CLLVIII, No. 2 (May 1992), 177-199.

Ritchie-Noakes, N. *Liverpool's Historic Waterfront*. London, 1984.

Ritchie-Noakes, N. and Clarke, M. "The Dock Engineer and the Development of the Port of Liverpool." In V.C. Burton (ed.), *Liverpool Shipping, Trade and Industry*. Liverpool, 1989.

Dock Promotion, Politics, Management

Anderson, G. "Inequalities in the Workplace: The Gap between Manual and White-Collar Workers in the Port of Liverpool from the 1850s to the 1930s." *Labour History Review*, LVI, No. 1 (Spring 1991), 36-48.

Jarvis, A. "Harold Littledale, the Man with a Mission." In H.M. Hignett (ed.), *A Second Merseyside Maritime History*. Liverpool, 1991.

Jarvis, A. "The Interests and Ethics of John Foster, Liverpool Dock Surveyor 1799-1824." *Transactions of the Historic Society of Lancashire and Cheshire*, CXL (1990), 141-160.

Jarvis, A. "Alfred Jones: Integration and Adversity in Liverpool." in L.R. Fischer (ed.), *From Wheelhouse to Counting House: Studies in Maritime Business History in Honour of Professor Peter Neville Davies*. St. John's, 1992.

Jarvis, A. "Liverpool Dock Engineers, Railways and Engineering Ethics." In *Nineteenth Century Business Ethics*. Liverpool, 1993.

Mountfield, S. *Western Gateway*. Liverpool, 1965.

Taplin, E. "Dock Labour at Liverpool, Occupational Structure and Working Conditions in the Late Nineteenth Century." *Transactions of the Historic Society of Lancashire and Cheshire*, CXXVII (1977), 133-154.

Contemporary Printed Material

A great deal of information about the Liverpool docks was published at the time. This is particularly true of the engineering aspects. *The Engineer and Engineering* can be found in most major libraries, and while they do not generally contain a wealth of detail, their indices make them excellent finding aids. They will, for example, index conferences whose proceedings you may find elsewhere, and patents which can be obtained at the Patent Office. Cumulative indexes were produced for the *Minutes of the Proceedings of the Institution of Civil Engineers* and the *Proceedings of the Institution of Mechanical Engineers* and both series will be found to contain important papers. Notable examples include G.F. Lyster, "Recent Dock Extensions at Liverpool," *Min. Proc. ICE*,

C (1889-1890), 2, and P. Westmacott, "Description of the Machinery for Warehousing Grain at the Liverpool Docks," *Proc. IME* (1869), 206. The special merit of these sources is that papers were open to the criticism of the author's peers, and in the case of *Min. Proc. ICE* and *Proc. IME*, the discussion and correspondence often amount to several times the length of the paper, giving the views, not always complimentary, of other professionals at the time.

Engineering, like other professions, needed a training system to perpetuate its skills. This in turn mandated textbooks and the better among these carefully relate the purely engineering aspects to the needs of a port's customers. In the Liverpool context, special mention should be made of the works of Brysson Cunningham, who served his pupillage in the Dockyard, but the notes and bibliography of I. Weir, "Port of Liverpool Quay Walls" (Unpublished MSc Dissertation, University of Liverpool, 1993) will provide many more examples.

The Upper Mersey Navigation Commission

This Commission was established by Act of Parliament in 1876. Its duties were the maintenance of lights and buoys on the upper estuary from a line between Garston and Eastham and Bank Quay, Warrington, for which it could levy dues. It was wound up in 1973. Some of its records are in private hands and these are referred to in Starkey, 232.

Records

Minute Books, 1876-1963; Ledgers, 1877-1955.
Dues received registers, 1903-1964.
Superintendent's Reports, 1904-1947.
Log Books of Commission's vessels, 1921.
Hale Lighthouse records, 1933-1958.
Misc. correspondence & papers from 1860, including brief history of UMNC.
Charts, c. 1870-c. 1970.
Reports of the Mersey Conservancy, 1878-1971.
UMNC   c. 1860-1971   30 boxes

Reference

Starkey, H.F. *Schooner Port*. Ormskirk, 1983, 114-116, 189, 206-207, 232.

CHAPTER 3

SHIPPING AND TRADE ASSOCIATIONS

Introduction

The nineteenth century, especially after 1850, was characterised by a multiplication of specialist trades and functions in ports and the shipping industry. This specialisation led to the rise of trade associations in Liverpool for shipping, distribution, marine insurance, port employment and the commodity trades. Some wielded enormous economic power. For example, the Liverpool Cotton Association's members handled about eighty percent of the country's cotton imports in their exchange. The records in the Maritime Museum provide a useful cross section of their activities, although there are large gaps. References to these associations, their members and matters such as port labour can also be found in the MDHB Collection and the Bryson Collection. The latter has extensive marine insurance records, as has the Danson Collection. The local marine insurance industry is also covered in the "Safe Passage" gallery on the third floor of the museum.

Ship Owners' Associations

British Liner Committee

This Committee was established jointly by the Chamber of Shipping and the Liverpool Steamship Owners' Association. There are three bound volumes of the Committee's reports and memoranda in the Bryson collection. These are available *strictly by appointment only.*

DB/115/p2 (and unnumbered)   1956-1960   3 Volumes

Canadian Atlantic Freight Secretariat

This was a shipping "Conference" set up in 1907 to control freight rates on cargo liner services between Canada and the United Kingdom. The first formal Conference was established in 1875 to regulate the Calcutta trade and the practice spread to other liner trades. This conference was based in Liverpool until its closure in 1985. Greenshields, Cowie and Co. (later McDiarmid

Greenshields and Co.) operated as merchants from about 1834 and later became shipowners and agents. From 1974 they were owned by the Crown Agents.

The Archives of shipowners contain a wide range of documents from conferences on other routes, for example in the Brocklebank, Ocean and PSNC Archives (see section 4).

Records

Calcutta Conference circulars, etc., 1879-1919; letters, 1907-1948; freight rates, 1879-1937.

Far East Conference minutes, Calcutta, 1898-1945; freight rates, Bombay, 1877-1913; Madras and Columbo, 1885; India, 1927-1937.

River Plate freight rates, 1901-1906; letters, 1898-1910.

Alexandria freight rates, 1928-1931.

Port Said freight fates, 1936-1937; minutes, 1927-1946.

Steam Trade Conference, London-India, 1885-1887.

East African Freight Commissions, 1913-1934.

Atlantic Eastbound Conference, New York circulars, etc., 1932-1941; minutes, 1919-1958.

North Atlantic and Canadian Westbound Freight Association, minutes, 1907-1930; selected letters, 1907-1974; agendas, 1919-1958; freight rates, 1905-1965.

North Atlantic-UK Freight Conference tariff, 1935-1967.

Ledgers, 1892-1949; other financial records, 1892-1963; rebate books, 1908-1948.

Contracts, Canadian, 1935-1968; USA, 1959.

Canadian Westbound Forwarding Association Ltd., Articles of Association, 1938.

Canadian Freight pooling agreement, 1885-1887.

Imperial Shipping Committee, North Atlantic Inquiry, 1926.

Report on North Atlantic Steamship Combine by W.T.R. Preston, 1924 (printed).

General letters, 1908-1945.

McDiarmid, Greenshields and Co., letters, 1891-1977.

Case papers, Aranji Line v. Anchor Line, 1958-1959, before Federal Maritime Board, USA.

Acts of Parliament, 1840-1919.

Board of Trade Regulations/Rules, 1896-1906.

Bulls' Iron & Steel Co., Liverpool, prospectus, paper on manufacture iron and steel, etc., 1882-1883.

Newscuttings, 1915-1926; 1935.

CAF   (1840) 1877-1977   123 Boxes

Reference

Burrell, D. "Fortunes of the Knight Line." *Sea Breezes*, New Series, LX (1980), 357-358.

Liverpool Ship Owners' Association

The Association was founded in 1810 to protect the interests of sailing ship owners in Parliament and elsewhere. In 1884 it formed a joint committee with the Liverpool Steamship Owners' Association and by 1895 represented about 800,000 tons of shipping, including steamers. In 1914 a substantial coastal steamship section was added. By 1928 the Association represented 182 steamers of 254,907 tons and one sailing ship of 100 tons; in 1988 it merged with the Liverpool Steamship Owners' Association.

No records survive before the Association's incorporation in 1888. Its records include those of two mutual insurance associations – the Liverpool Shipowners' Freight, Demurrage and Defence Association Ltd. and the Liverpool Sailing Ship Owners' Mutual Protection and Indemnity Association Ltd. These were established to protect members' uninsured risks. There was also a Liverpool Sailing Ship Owners' Mutual Indemnity Association in 1889, which was probably the forerunner of the latter association. A list of its members is in the DX collection. The records also contain the minutes of the Garston Docks Joint Shipowners' and Coal Shippers' Committee which reflects the importance of coasting members. The records are available *strictly by appointment*.

Records

Memorandum and articles of association, 1888.
Minutes 1906-1940.
Letter Books, 1937-1960.
Register books and files (Companies Act), c. 1939-1957.
Cash Book, 1889-1914.
Accounts Book (Bank of Liverpool), 1902-1914.
Parliamentary Committee reports, 1922 and 1926.
The Liverpool Shipowners' Freight, Demurrage and Defence Association Ltd., minutes, 1895-1901, 1906-1917.
Articles of Association, 1895; certificate of incorporation, 1895.
Subscription and expenses account book, 1895-1917.
Liverpool Sailing Ship Owners' Mutual Protection and Indemnity Association Ltd., memorandum and articles of association, 1894.
Annual Report, 1893-1894.
List of sailing vessels, 1894.

Garston Docks Joint Shipowners' and Coal Shippers' Committee, minutes, 1940-1948.

Miscellaneous

Chamber of Shipping of the United Kingdom Documentary Committee rules, 1909, and other material.
Report of Joint Committee of Chamber of Shipping and the Liverpool Steamship Owners' Association re: sub-division of passenger vessels, 1921.
D/S   1888-1960   10 Boxes

Reference

Fletcher, H.F. "Shipowners' Organisations" in J.A. Todd (ed.). in *The Shipping World*. London, 1929.

The Liverpool Steamship Owners' Association

The Liverpool Steamship Owners' Association was established in 1858 mainly to secure representation of steamship interests on the new MDHB. It attracted a substantial membership from leading liner companies and as a result became influential in national as well as local affairs and was consistently consulted by parliamentary committees on the shipping industry. At the time, the total tonnage of British steamers was a mere 381,000 tons (less than ten percent), compared with 4.2 million tons for all British shipping. Six shipowners formed the founding committee, representing 70,000 tons of shipping. By 1958 the membership was sixty-seven, representing 4,631,240 tons. In 1988 the Association merged with the Liverpool Ship Owners' Association. That same year Ocean Transport and Trading, once the largest member shipping company, having sold its deep-sea shipping interests, resigned. The Association since changed its name to the Liverpool Steam Ship Owners' and Agents' Association.

The minute books contain not only a detailed account of each meeting but also all correspondence sent to the Association, reports and memoranda (confidential, unofficial and official), annual reports of the Association and every piece of legislation (and associated documents) having a bearing on the mercantile marine. Correspondents include the Board of Trade, Lloyds of London, chambers of commerce, overseas steamship owners' associations and harbour and port authorities around the world. Subjects covered include imports (especially cotton and grain), commodity prices, bills of lading, marine insurance, unionised dock labour, safety at sea, policing of the world's navigable rivers and the ice code. Documentation for the two World Wars is particularly thorough. There is additional material in the Bryson Collection. The whole collection has recently been microfilmed and will be available commercially.

Records

Minute Books, 1858-1964.
Printed Annual reports, bound volumes, 1859-1961.
Loose issues, 1962-1989.
Miscellaneous reports, 1890-1965.
Centenary history, 1958.
Miscellaneous papers, 1937-1945.
D/SS   1858-1989   100 Boxes and Volumes

Reference

Powell, L.H. *History of the Liverpool Steamship Owners' Association, 1858-1958.* Liverpool, 1958.

Employers' Associations

Employers' Labour Association

This was formed in 1890 by employers of all types of port labour in response to the increasing disturbance to shipping caused by the dockers' and seamen's unions. It negotiated with the unions and from 1896 worked in close association with the Shipping Federation. By 1913, it had declined from fifty to thirteen members and was largely supplanted by the newly formed Employers' Association of the Port of Liverpool.

Records

Minutes, 1896-1931 (with agreement with Shipping Federation, 1896).
Cash book, 1890-1959
Ledger and journal, 1890-1967; financial statements, tonnage reports, etc., 1894-1965.
D/ELA   1890-1968   4 Boxes

References

Taplin, E.L. *Liverpool Dockers and Seamen 1870-1890.* Hull 1974.
Waller, P.J. *Democracy and Sectarianism: A Political and Social History of Liverpool, 1868-1939.* Liverpool, 1981.

Shipping Federation, Liverpool and Mersey District

This was a national association set up in 1890 to protect shipowners' interests against growing union unrest. Its chief members were protection and indemnity associations (though not the Liverpool and London P. and I. Association) acting on behalf of their shipowner members. The Federation divided the country into districts, of which Liverpool and the Mersey was one. Its main function was to provide indemnity against claims and assistance in time of strikes, to help obtain crews, to deal with claims on members under the Workmen's Compensation Act, to train seamen and to represent members at the National Maritime Board.

Reference

Fletcher, H.F. "Shipowners' Organisations" in J.A. Todd (ed.). *The Shipping World*. London, 1929, 152-159.

National Maritime Board

In 1917 the Ministry of Shipping requested the Seafarers' Committee of the Employers' Association of the port of Liverpool to advise them on all questions arising between owners and crews. This informal arrangement led to the establishment of the National Maritime Board to oversee the pay and conditions on ships. The Liverpool Association was not represented until 1919 because it disagreed with the Board's original constitution. The revised board was composed of sixty shipowners' representatives and an equal number from the trade unions, with five panels for masters, navigating officers, engineer officers, sailors and firemen and catering crew. The panels drew their representatives from district committees based on the major ports. The Board provided a national forum for the negotiation of pay and conditions in the shipping industry.

Records

National minutes (duplicate), 1939-1966.
Liverpool District Sailors' and Firemen's Panel, 1920-1950.
D/NMB   1920-1966   15 Boxes

Reference

Fletcher, H.F. "Shipowners' Organisations" in J.A. Todd (ed.). *The Shipping World*. London, 1929, 152-159.

Records

Liverpool, minutes, 1893-1920.
Mersey, minutes, 1896-1911; 1920-1928; 1942-1966.
Photographs, mobile canteen, 1944; seamen signing on, 1958; album, National
Sea Training Schools, Trafalgar Dock, 1968.
D/SF   1893-1968   2 Boxes

Reference

Fletcher, H,F. "Shipowners' Organisations" in J.A. Todd (ed.). *The Shipping
World*. London, 1929, 152-159.

Employers' Association of the Port of Liverpool

The serious industrial disturbances of 1911 saw the creation of Joint Committees
in Liverpool for settling disputes in the transport industry and led to the
foundation of the Employers' Association of the Port of Liverpool in 1914. The
Association appears to have been known initially as the Shipping Employers'
Association. Under its revised title its membership encompassed most dock
work, including shipowners, repairers, tug and barge owners, stevedores, master
carters and porters. There were four permanent committees: the Dock Labour
Committee, the Dock Labour Organisation Committee, the Seafarers' Committee
and the Shipowners' General Labour Committee. The boxed files accompanying
the minutes contain some files for the committees. The recent files are still
confidential.

Records

Minutes, 1913-1987.
Boxed files, c. 1930-1987 (mainly 1940 onwards).
Dock Labour Joint Committee minutes, 1911-1978.
Dock Labour Organisation Committee minutes, 1915-1963.
D/PEA   1911-1987   22 Volumes, 227 Boxes

Seafarers' Joint Committee minutes, 1914-1917.
Seafarers' Joint Committee Employers' Representatives minutes, 1914-1966.
D/SJ   1914-1966   4 Volumes 2 Boxes

Marine Insurance Associations

Liverpool Association of Average Adjusters

In marine insurance "general average" is the sacrifice of property (cargo or vessel) in time of danger for the ultimate safety of the whole enterprise. The average adjuster was a specialist responsible for advising, negotiating and settling marine insurance claims especially those under "general average" clauses which could be very difficult and complex. Sir Francis Danson (see Danson collection) was a pioneer in establishing average adjusting as a profession and took a leading role in the Liverpool and the national associations.

Records

Minute books, annual conferences, rules, meeting with Liverpool Chamber of
         Commerce, resolutions of International Maritime Conference, letters.
DX/41   1882-1916   1 Box

Reference

Biglands, J.R. "Marine Insurance." *Transactions of the Liverpool Nautical
       Research Society*, VIII (1953-1955), 47-60.

Liverpool and London Steam Ship Protection and Indemnity Association

The restriction of the collision claims to three-quarters of a vessel's value was designed to prevent shipowners from conspiring to sink their own ships. Ship-owners had to find a quarter of a claim and they joined together in mutual associations or "clubs" to protect themselves. The Liverpool and London Steam Ship Protection and Indemnity Association was set up in 1881 by leading Liverpool shipowners including White Star, Cunard and Blue Funnel. These records are part of the Bryson Collection and are still being catalogued. They include a few letter books of the 1950s, accounts 1883-1905, 1930-1940, and miscellaneous papers from the Second World War. They are available *strictly by appointment only*.

Records

D/B(unnumbered)   c.1883-1953   6 Boxes

Liverpool and London War Risks Insurance Association

This was a mutual association formed by Sir Norman Hill of the Liverpool marine solicitors Hill, Dickinson, in 1913. It covered members' vessels in time of war when Great Britain was neutral and until their ships arrived in a safe port after war had been declared. These records (part of the Bryson Collection) are still being catalogued and are available *strictly be appointment*. The bulk of the Archives is still held by Hill, Dickinson.

Records

D/B/115F (and unnumbered)   1914-1945   11 Boxes

D/B/115AA, BB Minutes of the Fund for the Advancement of Officers' Children, 1918-1928 - 2 Boxes

Reference

Kirkaldy, A.W. *British Shipping*. London, 1914, 255-256.

Liverpool Underwriters Association

The Liverpool Underwriters Association was founded by underwriters, brokers, merchants and shipowners at a public meeting held in the Exchange Coffee Room, Liverpool, on 8 January 1802, their purpose being the promotion and protection of their common commercial interests and those of the port of Liverpool. The organisation was the first of its kind in England. It enjoyed a close relationship with Lloyds and the Institute of London Underwriters, supplying both with information on Liverpool shipping.

The records of the L.U.A., particularly the Committee Minute Books (1802-1982) and the Annual Reports (1864-1972), show that the Association was concerned with all aspects of Liverpool shipping, navigation and legislation in order to minimise their risks. In 1835 the Association set up its own register of ships which merged with Lloyds' Register in 1846. Dissatisfaction with Lloyds' rules on iron ship construction led to the establishment of a separate register for iron vessels in 1862.

In addition to the three deposits of the Association's records in 1982, 1986 and 1992, there are copies of the Iron Ship Register and the 1835 and 1842 Liverpool registers in the Library.

Records

Committee minutes, 1802-1982.

Annual reports, 1864-1972.
Letter books, 1819-1918.
Subscription books, 1882-1969
L.U.A. casualty returns and reports, 1911-1985.
Company history files, 1872-1983.
Membership records, c. 1809-1963.
Yearbooks, 1892-1894.
Miscellaneous documents including policy for SS *Great Britain*, 1857,
     1808-1976.
Charts of the world showing soundings, c. 1810-1940.

Trade Associations

Liverpool Cold Storage Association

Rising living standards in Britain in the late nineteenth century encouraged an expansion in demand for meat. This was met at first by the importation of live cattle from Ireland and North America. The development of refrigeration made it possible to deliver frozen carcasses over long distances. From the first Australian shipment in 1879 the trade developed rapidly and by 1902 there were 147 British vessels in the frozen meat trade. The trade required shoreside refrigerated storage. At Liverpool, which came to account for a fifth of the trade, these included the Alexandra Dock cold store and the present Maritime Museum building at Albert Dock which was converted in 1899. The Bryson Collection contains the minutes of the Association.

Records

D/B/110A Minutes   1918-1941   1 Volume

The Liverpool Corn Trade Association

This Association was set up in 1886 as successor to the Association of the Liverpool Corn Trade founded in 1853. British grain imports for the growing urban population rose rapidly after the abolition of the Corn Laws in 1849. Liverpool had a major role as an importing and flour milling centre, especially for North American grain. The Association regulated the Liverpool Corn Exchange, which included a wheat futures market, information and arbitration services and an insurance scheme. It also traded maize and other animal feedstuffs. Its volume of trade was so great that it was regarded as a barometer of world wheat prices. Many of its Archives were destroyed in the blitz of 1941.

Records

Board meetings, 1916-1959; reports and accounts (incomplete), 1880-1981; register of tenders, 1937-1973; minutes of Clearing House Committee, 1924-1941; Grading Committee, 1903-1939; New Members Committee, 1910-1932; Standards Committee, 1907-1926; arbitration and appeals, 1912-1957; shareholders registers, 1897-1964; photographs, 1897-1971.

Liverpool Grain Contract Insurance Co., minutes, 1940-1964; report and accounts 1949; returns to company house, 1902-1964.

Liverpool Corn Trade Guild, minutes, 1955-1971.

Liverpool Corn Trade Clerks' Guild, annual reports and accounts, 1978-1983.

Liverpool Commodity Trades Association, directors' meetings minutes, 1981-1982; balance sheet and accounts, 1981-1982.

Corn Trade News, 1923-1968 (with gaps).

D/CORN   1858-1983   52 Boxes, 158 Volumes

Reference

The Port of Liverpool Handbook. Liverpool, 1937-1938, 120-121.

Liverpool Cotton Association

Raw cotton was the single most important import for Liverpool by 1850 and the city was the centre for the world trade in raw cotton. The Liverpool Cotton Association was the first to develop a "futures" market to allow buyers to secure future supplies at a fixed price. It also developed rules of trading and arbitration and standards of quality that were adopted world-wide. The decline of the Lancashire textile industry after the Second World War has reduced the Association's activities mainly to an information and arbitration service and its grand Edwardian Exchange Building of 1906 in Tithebarn Street was demolished in 1967. One of its cotton trading rings is displayed in the Museum of Liverpool Life, together with film of the Exchange's interior.

The Association's records held by the museum are a miscellaneous selection in the Bryson Collection.

Records

D/B/110M, minutes of Cotton Porters Employers' Committee, 1917-1931.

D/B/110Q, minutes of American Cotton Import Committee, 1917-1939.

D/B/110Q/111R, Liverpool Cotton Association, minutes of the Enemy Debts Committee, 1920-1922; Bankruptcy proceedings re: cotton brokers 1898; Report of conference with Cotton Spinners' Association, 1899.

D/B/111Q, minutes of Cotton Control Board, raw cotton section, 1939-1940.

Liverpool Provision Trade Association

This association, founded in 1874, was first concerned with the produce of the American meat packing industry. After merging with the Liverpool Produce Exchange in 1889, it covered all imported pig and dairy produce, eggs and canned goods. Its exchange provided a "trading floor" and in 1912 it added a lard futures market. Its objectives were to foster overseas trading, to publish information on markets, to arbitrate disputes and to represent the trade in negotiations with other organisations. Its trading rules became standard.

Records

Minute books with annual reports, 1874-1889, 1914-1920, 1955-1977; rules, 1930, 1937, 1958; cash books, 1945-1975; various items of ephemera including a souvenir of the opening of the New Produce Exchange in Liverpool, 1902.

D/PTA   1874-1977   6 Boxes

Reference

The Port of Liverpool Handbook. Liverpool, 1937-1938, 122-123.

The Sugar Association of Lancashire

The association, founded in 1882, comprised all the sugar refineries and brokers in the port. It was wound up in 1981 and the London Sugar Association took over its responsibilities.

Records

Minute books, 1882-1969; letters, 1894-1901, 1929-1966; legal records, 1886-1891; financial records, 1887-1981; operational records, 1966-1981; personnel documents, 1929-1980; miscellaneous, 1885-1981.

D/SAL   1882-1981   16 Boxes

CHAPTER 4

SHIPOWNERS

Introduction

A large proportion of this section has come from the major steamship companies of Liverpool: Ocean, Elder Dempster, Pacific Steam Navigation Co., Ellerman, Lamport and Holt and Brocklebank are all prominent and date from the late nineteenth and twentieth centuries. Even with the loss of a large number of vessels in both world wars Liverpool remained a major, though declining, centre for shipowning into the 1970s, and the acquisition of these collections is linked with the closure of offices and the sale of ships. The bulk of the ships were passenger and cargo liners as opposed to tramps, bulk carriers or tankers. From the mid-1960s there were moves to join consortia to fund the establishment of container services and diversification into other ship types, such as gas tankers.

Apart from the Brocklebank collection, there is little material on the sailing ship owners who owned a higher proportion of Liverpool's tonnage until the mid-1880s. To an extent their activities can be traced through some of the collections listed in volume 2 – Merchants and other Maritime Businesses. Their ships are well documented through the Liverpool Registers of merchant ships, Lloyds and other commercial registers and personal research papers of sailing ship historians such as Captains Beard and Woods. The same applies to coasting companies and many of the passenger/cargo lines which did not survive into the mid-twentieth century; for example, the White Star Line records seem to have disappeared after the merger with Cunard in 1934, and as a result of this many other companies are represented by fragments. Other mergers have left some companies' records embedded in others. This is especially true for the Archives of the Ocean Group. Other collections within the Archives can also yield useful information, especially MDHB, Liverpool Steam Ship Owners Association, solicitors' accumulations such as Alsop Wilkinson, and the Bryson collection. It should also be noted that most major companies have a published history (of varying quality) and these are useful starting points. Other local collections are also important, especially the Liverpool City Record Office and the University of Liverpool Archives, which holds the bulk of the Cunard Archives.

For an overview of Liverpool shipowning business, the following are particularly useful:

79

Cottrell, P.L. "The Steamship in the Mersey 1815-1880, Investment and Ownership." In P.L. Cottrell and D.H. Aldcroft (eds.), *Shipping, Trade and Commerce, Essays in Memory of Ralph Davis*. Leicester, 1981, 137-163.

Hyde, F.E. *Liverpool and the Mersey, the Development of the Port, 1700-1970*. Newton Abbot, 1971.

Neal, F. "Liverpool Shipping in the Early 19th Century," In J.R. Harris (ed.), *Liverpool and Merseyside. Essays in the Economic History of the Port and Its Hinterland*. London, 1969, 147-181.

African Steamship Co.

The company was founded in 1852 by MacGregor Laird (1808-1861), a relative of the Birkenhead shipbuilders and explorer of the Niger. It ran a cargo, mail and passenger service to West Africa from London until 1875 when it moved to Liverpool. In 1890 it was taken over by its main competitor, Elder Dempster. It should be noted that these records have been incorporated into the general body of the Ocean Steam Ship Co.'s records. MacGregor Laird's own correspondence (1848-59) and family papers are in a separate collection, DX/258. The museum holds a model of the *Ethiope*, 1854.

Records

Reports (printed), 1853-1923.
Rates of freight, 1929.
OA   1853-1929   4 Volumes

Reference

Davies, P.N. *The Trade Makers Elder Dempster in West Africa 1852-1972*. London, 1973.

Alexandra Towing Co. Ltd.

Founded at Liverpool in 1887, after the take-over of G.B. Cowl's towage firm of 1882, with the Mack family (see J.J. Mack and Co.) and Alexander Bicket (Athel Line) among the major shareholders, it became one of the major towage firms on the Mersey. It took over W. & T. Joliffe and Co. of Liverpool, a tug company founded in 1854. In 1919 it followed the Cunard Line's move to Southampton and in 1925 it had a base at Swansea. A series of takeovers between 1962 and 1975 including Liverpool Screw Towing, Britannia Towing

Co. (Swansea) in 1962, J.H. Lamey in 1968 and London Tugs in 1975, made it a national business. It also diversified into deep-sea towage, offshore services, ship repair, aircraft and road transport. In 1992 it was sold to Howard Smith Industries of Hull. The museum holds a number of plans in the SAS collection, five models and the full size tug *Brocklebank* (1964). Detailed lists of the other "subsidiary companies," listed at the end, are available on application.

Records

Corporate/administration records, 1887-1977: minute books, 1887-1966; letterbooks, correspondence, 1954-1977.

Investment records, 1893-1979: share ledgers, certificates, etc.

Financial (including insurance) 1887-1990: annual reports, 1967-1990; profit and loss accounts, 1908-1972; working papers 1980-1985; accounts ledgers, 1887-1981; cash books, 1922- 1956.

Operational 1966-1985: quotation books, 1900-1910; daybooks, 1966-1968; logbooks, 1967-1984; damage statements, 1973-1980.

Staff 1901-1969: registers of directors, 1901, 1948-1959; records of employment, 1947-1960; wage books, 1927-1966; wages file, 1961; injuries and accident file, 1963-1969.

Publicity, Miscellaneous 1912-1984: newscuttings, c. 1950-1979; promotional brochures, leaflets, c. 1960s; history files, c. 1980s.

Photographs 1912-1984: photographs of tugs and other vessels relating to all associated companies.

Records of Other Companies included in the Archives: Alexandra Marine Transportation Ltd., 1982-1984; Britannia Steam Towage Ltd., 1935-1972; Bulk Cargo Handling Services, 1963-1981; Drysdale Towing Ltd., 1964; J.H. Lamey Ltd., c. 1946-1967; Liverpool Screw Towing Ltd., 1909-1968; Medway Dry Dock and Engineering Co. Ltd., 1983-1984; North West Tugs Ltd., 1895-1966; Southampton Steamship Co. Ltd., 1933; United Grain Elevators Ltd., c. 1900.
B/AT   1887-1990   46 Boxes, 75 Volumes

Reference

Nicholson, T. *Take the Strain, The Alexandra Towing Company and the British Tugboat Business, 1833-1937.* Liverpool, 1990.

Allan Line

The Montreal Ocean Steamship Co. (popularly known as the Allan Line) was founded by Hugh Allan in 1854 to provide a regular steamship service from Liverpool to Canada. Early successes included winning the Canadian mail contract in 1856 and attracting a substantial emigrant traffic by direct sailings from Glasgow with calls at Irish ports. It also managed to survive the wreck of eight of its ships between 1857 and 1864. In spite of intense competition, the Line was successful on its Canadian routes and had a fleet of twenty-two ships at the time of its founder's death in 1883. In 1897 the company was restructured as the Allan Line Steamship Company Ltd. to provide capital for new ships. Competition from the International Mercantile Marine from 1902 and Canadian Pacific Railway Company from 1903 led to amalgamation with Canadian Pacific in 1915. It was often technically innovative and its *Victorian* and *Virginian* of 1905 were the first steam turbine liners.

The records are a miscellany in the DX collection except for the records of its benefit society, which are complete.

Records

Publicity brochure, 1900.
Notebook of ships and voyages, 1892-1893.
Sailing posters, 1886-1911.
Passenger list, 1913.
Miscellaneous wreck papers, 1863.
Minute books, nomination books, annual reports, etc. for the Montreal O.S.S.
        Co. Mutual Benefit Society, c.1863-1966
SAS/23D/1-3 & DX various   c. 1863-1966   1 Box

Reference

Appleton, T.E. *Ravenscrag. The Allan Royal Mail Line.* Toronto, 1974.

Anchor Line

The Anchor Line was founded by Thomas Henderson and the Handyside Brothers to provide a Glasgow-New York steamer service. From 1866 its weekly service called at Moville for Irish emigrants. In 1869 Scandinavian emigrants began to be carried on a feeder service to Leith and onwards by rail to Glasgow. In 1871 it developed a Mediterranean-US service and its *Dido* was the first British steamer to pass through the Suez Canal in 1869. From this it developed a cargo service to Bombay and Calcutta. From 1873 it became a regular customer of the Barrow Shipbuilding Co. and was involved in the unsuccessful attempt to develop Barrow as a transatlantic port. In 1882 it took over the liner *City of Rome* which had been handed back to its builders by the Inman Line. It was used to start a Liverpool-New York service.

In the years after the dates of the records listed below the line underwent many changes including: 1911, purchase by Cunard and Brocklebank's takeover of the Indian service; 1916, merger with Donaldson for a Canadian service; purchase by Runciman in 1935; purchase by United Molasses in 1953; and re-sale to Runciman in 1965. The Cunard collection contains Anchor Line ship plans and the Brocklebank collection has charter parties, 1911-1936.

Records

Ship's newspaper, *City of Rome Express* (Liverpool-New York), 1890. SAS/29/2/3

Headed notepaper (2 unused sheets) SAS/33E/1/1

Poster: Liverpool-New York colour illustration of ship *Furnessia*, steerage fare and plan of salon and cabin, 1892
DX/1169

Reference

McLellan, R.S. *Anchor Line 1856-1956*. Glasgow, 1956.

Associated Container Transportation Ltd.

Five British companies – Ben, Blue Star, Cunard, Ellerman and Harrison – formed Associated Container Transport (ACT) in 1966 to invest in container ships for their European-Australian services. Associated Container Transport (Australia) [ACT(A)], set up in 1967, pioneered refrigerated containers to provide a service for the important Australian meat trade. These printed items came from the Vestey Group offices in Liverpool.

Records

ACTA News, 1973.

ACT News, 1973-1991.
ACT Container News, 1974-1975.
CONTACTS (House Journal of Associated Container Transportation Services
        Ltd.), 1974-1985.
ACT TODAY, 1971-1980.
ACTION LINE (Newsletter of Act(A) (Australia) and Shipping Corporation of
        New Zealand Ltd.), nd.
CONTACT ACTA (Australia), 1980-1989.
ACT GENERAL (Publicity brochure), c.1969-1988, *The World of Act*, 1975,
        1980; *History of the Service*, 1990.
Miscellaneous, including photographic prints, 1970-1990.
CONTAINERISATION INTERNATIONAL (monthly, including special reports),
        1975-1991.
CARGO WARE INTERNATIONAL, April-December 1989.
OCL (Overseas Containers Ltd.), 1969-1989.
COMPASS News (Report from the Port of Liverpool), June-September 1986.
JOURNAL OF COMMERCE (Supplement), 1981-1984.
Miscellaneous brochures, 1971-1983.
B/ACT   1969-1991   6 Boxes

Athel Line

The British Molasses Company was founded in Liverpool by J.H. Clayton, a
Liverpool produce importer, and Michael Kroyer-Kielberg, a Dane, in 1915.
Alexander Bicket (of Alexandra Towing) was also on the Board. The company
went through various changes, becoming United Molasses Company Ltd., with
its head office in London, in 1926. It specialised in the bulk carriage and storage
of molasses. The company acquired its first ship in 1921 and soon bought an
American Great Lakes steamer re-named *Athelstane*. Thereafter all of the names
of its ships bore the prefix "Athel." The company was acquired by Tate and
Lyle in 1965.

It is not known where other records of the shipping side of this
company are. These few items were presented by Captain W.A. Meneight of
Formby, the historian of the company. The company owned the Anchor Line
from 1949 to 1965. The museum holds models of the *Athelprince*, 1926, and the
Athelcrown, 1929.

Records

Volume of charter parties, 1936-1942.
Athel News (house journal), 2 vols., 1969-1976.
DX/255   1936-1976   1 Box, 1 Parcel

Reference

Meneight, W.A. *A History of United Molasses Ltd.* Liverpool, 1977.

Beaver Line

Founded by a group of Montreal merchants in 1867 as the Canadian Shipping Company to run fast iron sailing ships from Liverpool to Montreal, it chose the beaver for its house flag. In 1874 the firm moved into steam. In 1898 Elder Dempster bought it, but in 1902 sold their Canadian interests to Canadian Pacific. Unfortunately, the early Elder Dempster records have been destroyed but Beaver Line material may exist within the Canadian Pacific records held by the Canadian National Archives.

The records of Captain Evans (see Canadian Pacific entry) cover his career during his Beaver Line service, and there are references in the MDHB and a file on a Beaver Line outward voyage in 1887-1888, including a tribute from a group of first-class passengers and the case of claim for damages of a passenger in the Bryson collection.

Records

DB/115/JJ   1887-1888   1 File

Reference

Bonsor, N.R.P. *North Atlantic Seaway. Vol.3.* Jersey, 1979, 1198-1220.

Bibby Line

In 1807 John Bibby and John Highfield, Liverpool shipbrokers, began taking shares in ships, mainly Parkgate-Dublin packets. By 1821 (the end of the partnership) they had vessels sailing to the Mediterranean and South America. In 1850 they expanded their Mediterranean and Black Sea interests by buying two steamers and by 1865 their fleet had increased to twenty-three. The opening of the Suez Canal in 1869 severely affected their business and Frederick Leyland, their general manager, failed to persuade the family partners to diversify onto the Atlantic. Eventually, he bought them out in 1873. In 1889 the Bibby family revived its shipowning interests with a successful passenger-cargo service to Burma. From 1893 it also began to carry British troops to overseas postings which remained a Bibby staple until 1962. The Burma service ended in 1971 and the company moved to new areas of shipowning including bulkers, gas tankers and accommodation barges. It still has its head office in Liverpool where most management records are held. The museum holds models of the *Staffordshire* (1929) and *Oxfordshire* (1955).

Records

Management: report on a visit to the east, re: cargo, passenger traffic and accommodation, 1936-1937.

Staff: records of engineers and officers, c. 1860-1955 (some of these records contain full cover profiles before joining the company).

Fleet: specifications for *Staffordshire, Worcestershire, Derbyshire, Devonshire, Leicestershire, Oxfordshire, Yorkshire, Dorsetshire*, and *Gloucestershire*, 1925-1957; logbooks for the Brig *Thames* (Liverpool-Brazil-Mayoumba; reference to visit on board of King Maburee in Mayoumba), 1812-1813; Brig *George the Fourth* (Hamburg-Brazil-Demerara-Rio de Janeiro-Hamburg-Liverpool), 1822-1824; *Mary Bibby* (Liverpool-Rio de Janeiro-Rotterdam), 1825-1826; *John Bibby* (Liverpool-Calcutta-Hong Kong), 1846-1847; modern logbooks, 1955-1969.

Miscellaneous

Insurance Book, Britain S.S. Co. Ltd., 1890-1965.
Book of Rememberance re: loss of MV *Derbyshire*, 1980.
Published works on marine engineering etc., 1888-1955; Ministry of Transport/Board of Trade/War Department, instructions etc. re: tonnage measurements, defence precautions, etc., 1928-1957; miscellaneous published works including firefighting on ships, 1949-1965; *Bibby Gazette*, 1973.
Modern Publicity Brochures, c. 1937-1991.
Photographs in files, including launch albums, c. 1950-1980.
Launch films: *Lincolnshire* (1972); *English Bridge* (1973).
B/Bibby   1812-1973   14 Boxes

Bibby/Parker Yachting Album, 1879-c.1950 DX/640

Reference

Bibby, Sir D.J. *Glimpses*. Liverpool, 1991.

Paget-Tomlinson, E.W. *Bibby Line: 175 Years of Achievement*. Liverpool, 1982.

Watson, N. *The Bibby Line, 1807-1990.* London, 1990.

Black Ball Line of Australian Packets

The Liverpool Black Ball Line of Australian Packets was started in 1852 by James Baines and Co. to carry emigrants and cargo at the height of the gold rush to Melbourne. Its first large vessel, *Marco Polo*, made a record-breaking roundtrip voyage in 1852 and the Line's reputation for fast passages. Its large clippers, built by Donald Mackay at Boston, attracted national attention.

The Gold Rush traffic declined after 1856 and the Line diversified by starting a service to Queensland and ran a joint service with the British and Australian Steam Navigation Co. In 1864 there was an unsuccessful attempt to merge with White Star and Gibbs, Bright and Co. of Liverpool. A year later the firm was involved in floating as a public company the bank from which it had borrowed heavily. In 1866, in one of the worst banking crises of the nineteenth century, the bank suspended payment. The Black Ball Line was one of its major debtors and was forced to sell many of its vessels, relying on chartered ships to maintain its sailings. By 1871 the Line had declined into financial ruin and there was an unsuccessful attempt to revive it in 1873. This Line took its name from the Liverpool-New York Black Ball Line of 1818 (see Cropper family collection, volume 2).

Records

Mortgages, receipts, letters, etc., between James Baines and Thomas Mackay and John Bonus of London re: ownership of *Elizabeth Ann Bright* and *Spirit of the North*, and salvage claims on the former vessel, cargoes, etc., 1860-1866.

Mortgage, receipts, correspondence, etc., re: purchase and operation of *Sydney Dacres*, 1864-1866; memorandum of agreement, account sheets and receipts re: *Castlemaine*, 1863-1867; assignment of freights and policies of insurance, certificates of registration, mortgage, etc., re: *Marco Polo*; also wages accounts, receipts for mooring, etc., for same vessel, 1862-1867.

Letters, receipts, memorandum of agreement re: sale of *Mayflower*, 1862-1863; indenture between James Baines and John Bonus, shipbroker of London re: insurance on the *Netherby*; mortgage, receipts for various vessels, and correspondence, newscuttings, etc., re: wreck of *Netherby*, Melbourne, Australia, 1861-1866.

Assignment, accounts, letters re: sale of *Prince Consort*, 1860; assignments and
      mortgage re: *Runnymede*, 1864-1865; assignment, mortgage, accounts
      and letters re: *Duke of Newcastle*, 1862.
B/Baines   1860-1867   1 Box

Items in miscellaneous collections SAS/DX:
Correspondence between James Baines and Co. and the Emigration Commis-
sioners re: outbreak of cholera on the *Conway*, 1854.
SAS/3/2/2 & DX 1017b

Ship's newspaper (photocopy), *Commodore Herald*, 1857, SAS/33E/1/2
Research notes including photocopies of logs and other records, business and
      ship details compiled by M.K. Stammers, author of *The Passage
      Makers*.
D/MKS   c. 1852-1871   2 Boxes

Reference

Stammers, M.K. *The Passage Makers. The History of the Black Ball Line of
      Australian Packets, 1852-1871*. Brighton, 1978.

The Booker Line

Josiah Booker, son of a Lancashire miller, started as a sugar planter in
Demerara (Guyana) in 1815. He set up a Liverpool office in 1832 and sent his
first ship to Demerara in 1835. In 1867 the firm started the "Liverpool Line"
as a regular direct service and in 1900 merged with McConnell, another sugar
firm. In 1911 it changed the name of its cargo liner service to the Booker Line
on the purchase of its first steamer. The company operated coastal vessels in
Guyana and in 1955 bought the Liverpool coasting shipowners, S. William Coe
& Co. and then Metcalf Motor Coasters in 1972. The Line continued after 1976
(when the company handed over its sugar interests to the government of
Guyana) until 1981. Coe-Metcalf, the British coasting fleet, was sold to J.
Fisher & Co. of Barrow, but still continues to run its ships from its Liverpool
office. The museum has three models on loan.

Records

Cargo books, 1954-1960; framed certificate of agreed monthly wages to John
      Wilson for intended service on sailing vessel *John Horrocks*, signed by
      Josias Booker, 1842; Crest presented on the christening of SS *Ama-
      kura*, 1949; Booker Line calendar with drawing of SS *Imataka*, 1913;

Letter from Booker Line re: landing storage and delivery charges at Georgetown, 1977.

Poster re: Booker Bros. McConnell contributions to British Guiana, c. 1950; B/W photograph of *Booker Valiance*, c. 1965; Pamphlets include – *A Modern Wharf for the Port of Georgetown*; *Bookers Shipping (Demerara Ltd.)*, and a history of the Booker Line, 1835-1978, reprinted from *Sea Breezes*, 1977.

B/BOK   c. 1842-1977   4 Boxes

Booker Vanguard, 1964 (article from *Shipping World*); and a brochure on the Booker Line's combi-service to the Eastern Caribbean, c. 1970, etc. (see volume 2, library).

Notes on the Booker family and business; items of shipping and passenger memorabilia for *Booker Vanguard* and business in British Guiana, etc., c. 1965, the Stubbs family collection (see volume 2). D/STU

Watercolour of George Booker's sugar plantation, c. 1830, Bryson collection (see volume 2). D/B 176C

Reference

Anon. "Georgetown, Demerrara-Direct" *Sea Breezes*, New Series, XVIII (1954), 192-205.

Booth Line

After a business apprenticeship with Lamport and Holt and then as a leather merchant, Alfred Booth, with his brother Charles, started a two-ship steam service from Liverpool to north Brazil and the Amazon in 1866. In 1881 it became a limited company with a substantial Holt (Ocean) shareholding; and by 1903 it dominated the Amazon trade after taking over the Red Cross Line and the Liverpool and Maranharn S.S. Co. Its cruises up the Amazon were a popular feature. Their fleet was reduced to four ships through enemy action during the Second World War and in 1946 it was taken over by the Vestey Group. It continued to run to north Brazil with chartered tonnage until 1989.

The bulk of its records are currently held in the Liverpool Record Office. The museum holds four models of its ships including the *Lanfranc* of 1884 and some paintings of the Line's Amazon cruises.

Records

Reports and balance sheets, 1902-1941; agreement and rules for the regulation of the sheds at east side of Brunswick Dock, being berths appropriated for steamers of R. Singlehurst & Co., Booth S.S. Co., and Liverpool & Maranham S.S. Co., 1886; voyage summaries, 1909-1960; sealed memorandum of agreement – Minister of War Transport and Lamport and Holt Line Ltd. to purchase *Empire Franklin* with delivery deferred until after cessation of hostilities for £172,000 with attached sealed memorandum re: transfer to other parties and cancellation of agreement, 1943-1945.

B/BOOTH   1886-1945   2 Boxes

References

Heaton, P.M. *Booth Line*. Newport, 1987.

John, A.H. *A Liverpool Merchant House*. London, 1959.

British and African Steam Navigation Co.

The British and African Steam Navigation was established in 1868 by John Dempster and Alexander Laird to run cargo and passenger steamer services from Glasgow via Liverpool to West Africa in competition with their former employer, the African Steam Ship Co. Competition from other lines brought about increasing co-operation between the two lines in the 1850s. By 1890 both were controlled by Alfred Jones' firm, Elder Dempster. The survival of these records within the Elder Dempster Archives is unusual because these documents were normally handed in to the Board of Trade at the end of each voyage.

Records

Logs, crews lists and agreements, 1869-1907.

OA   1869-1907

Reference

Davies, P.N. *The Trade Makers. Elder Dempster in West Africa 1852-1972.* London, 1973.

Thomas and John Brocklebank Ltd.

This firm was one of the oldest in shipping, dating to 1801 when the two sons of the founder of the business took control following his death. The founder was Captain Daniel Brocklebank, a shipmaster and shipbuilder, whose shipbuilding enterprise was first established at Sheepscutt (near Portland, Maine) in 1770. Brocklebank was a Loyalist and when the Revolution broke out in 1775 he sailed back to Whitehaven in his own ship, *Castor* (its letter of marque of 1779 is the earliest document). He re-started his shipbuilding business at Whitehaven in 1785 and the plans and specifications of his yard's products from 1792 are one of the most important sources for eighteenth- and early nineteenth-century merchant ships. By 1795 his fleet consisted of eleven vessels of 1750 tons. The firm suffered somewhat in the Napoleonic wars but by 1809 it was sending ships as far as South America. By 1815 the fleet totalled seventeen ships. In 1815 the *Princess Charlotte*'s maiden voyage to Calcutta was a success following the end of the East India Company's monopoly. An estimate of its return freight suggested more than £10,000 in profits for her owners and other merchants. This trade eventually eclipsed Brocklebank's South American and China trades.

In 1819 Thomas Brocklebank moved to Liverpool and opened an office there in 1822. In 1829 Brocklebank began trading to China. In 1843 Thomas made his forty-year-old cousin Ralph a partner (later to become chairman of MDHB), and also his nephew Thomas Fisher, who took the name Brocklebank and was politically and socially active, becoming a Baronet in 1885. By 1844 the fleet had peaked at fifty vessels. The Whitehaven shipyard was closed in 1865 and larger iron and steel sailing ships were bought mainly from Harland and Wolff, Belfast. The first steamer, *Ameer*, was not purchased until 1889.

In 1911 Brocklebank ceased to be a family business. A substantial shareholding was sold to Sir Percy, Frederic and Denis Bates, grandsons of Sir Edward Bates who had built up an Indian trading firm. In the same year Cunard acquired the Anchor Line, which retained its independence and in turn gained a controlling interest in Brocklebank in 1912. The Bates brothers, Sir Alfred Booth and Sir Thomas Royden strengthened the business under the chairmanship of Sir Aubrey Brocklebank. In 1916 the Well Line was acquired and in 1919 Cunard bought out the Brocklebank and Bates shares; the final one-fifth shareholding held by Anchor Line was acquired in 1940. The firm experimented with motor ships including, for a short time, the first all-welded vessel, the coaster *Fullagar* of 1920. The shipping depression of the 1930s saw a reduction in the size of four of its ships in 1935 – a unique operation at the time. Sixteen of twenty-six ships were lost in the Second World War, including the *Malakand*, which blew up with an ammunition cargo in Liverpool in 1941. The fleet was rebuilt and services extended because of the decline of business at Calcutta after Indian independence in 1948. In 1964 it bought H.E. Moss and Co., tanker owners, and in 1967 Cunard Line became responsible for the passenger business and a new Cunard Brocklebank company took over all cargo services, including two Cunard-owned container ships in the Atlantic Container Lines consortium. The Brocklebank collection is varied and includes not only shipping business but family papers and research notes on the history compiled by J.S. Rees, which were used by J.F. Gibson for the company history. There are also excellent photographs, paintings (especially extensive for the sailing ships, 1815-1891) and models (1854-1946), which make the collection of national importance.

Records

Administration

Minutes of Directors' meeting, 1898-1963.
Annual General Meetings, 1918-1965; Executive Committee, 1912-1961.
Letterbooks (Whitehaven), 1801-1841, 1852-1863.
Private letterbook (Liverpool), 1888-1907.
Letter book of Denis H. Bates, 1912-1919.
Letters of Thomas Harrison to Captain Daniel Brocklebank, re: privateering, new ships, etc., 1782.
Business letters 1825-1829, 1861-1864.
File re: Thomas Brocklebank's chairmanship of Liverpool, London and Globe Insurance Co., 1874.

Legal

Lease of Bransty (Whitehaven) Ropeworks 1775; conveyance of Isaac Littledale & Co.'s ropeworks at Whitehaven to Daniel Brocklebank, 1749.
Partnership agreements, 1843, 1892.
Articles of association, 1898-1948.
Heads of agreement between T. & J. Brocklebank and Anchor Line, 1912, with correspondence, accounts, articles of association, 1907-1922.
Correspondence re: liquidation of Anchor Line and tax situation, 1935-1942.
Memorandum and articles of association of Well Line, with agreement for sale to T. & J. Brocklebank, 1916.
Papers re: war compensation court cases, against Ministry of Shipping, 1921, and Inland Revenue, 1923-1925.
Seal book, 1898-1948.
Agreements for sale and construction of ships, 1810, 1811, 1812.

Investment

Scrip book, 1898-1912.
Debenture holders' minute book, 1912.

Companies Act registers, 1900, 1903-1906, 1911-1919, 1948.
Register of mortgages and debentures, 1907-1921.
Register of transfers – debenture issue, 1907-1921.
Register of applications and allotments, 1911-1945.
Correspondence with Treasury re: issuing of shares, 1951.

Finance

Ledgers (Whitehaven), 1808-1855.
Cash books (Whitehaven), 1833-1860.
Cashiers' Office letterbooks, 1882-1905.
Loan book, 1900-1924.
Register of bills payable, 1929-1947.
Private ledger, 1938-1943.
Valuation of assets, 1921-1954.
Correspondence and accounts re: Excess Profits Duty obsolescence claims,
        share holdings, profit and loss accounts Income Tax, 1920-1931.
Correspondence with accountants, 1937-1941.
Ledger containing calculations of pre- and postwar profitability, 1919-1939.

Management

Reports on Japanese and Korean Ports, agency arrangements, etc., 1908.
Reports re: Bombay, 1920-1921.
Reports on Suez, Aden and Calcutta, 1931.
Report on Calcutta agency, 1933-1934.
Report on visit to India and Sri Lanka, 1948-1949.
Reports on overseas visits, 1950 and 1960 (including India, Pakistan and Sri
        Lanka).
Reports on visits to French, USA, Canadian ports, 1959.
File re: Calcutta Conference, 1916.
Correspondence and reports of Liverpool Steam Ship Owners' Association,
        (Denis H. Bates, Chairman), 1931-1937.
Report re: carrying Indian railways cargo, 1879, with correspondence, 1925.
Reports re: disagreements on homeward berths at Calcutta for Dundee,
        1922-1934.
Continental Conference Agreement negotiations, reports, etc., 1930.
Chairman's notes for speech on British shipping, 1936.
Report on Shipping Conference, 1944.
File re: National Maritime Board rates of pay 1947.
Memorandum of meeting with competitors, 1950.
Correspondence on malpractices, 1958.

Correspondence on Calcutta Conferences, Calcutta operations and T.J.
Harrison, 1957-1959.
Reports by Chamber of Shipping and Liverpool Steamship Owners Association,
1960.

Operational

Letter of Marque to Daniel Brocklebank for privateering against Spain in ship
Castor, 1779.
Store book, 1895-1899.
Notebooks of ship movements, 1907-1932.
Schedule, Anchor Brocklebank Line, 1912.
Notebooks of voyage details, 1931-1950.
Anchor-Brocklebank Charter Parties, 1911-1936.
Correspondence re: berthing arrangements of T. and J. Harrison and T. and J.
Brocklebank at Liverpool, 1950-1957.

Staff

Whitehaven apprentice book, 1809-1840.
Liverpool apprentice books, 1820-1897.
Officers and apprentices books, 1851-1900.
Officers and engineers books, 1891-1923.
Sea staff index, c. 1890-1920.
Seaman's apprenticeship indenture, 1787.
Letter of instruction to Captain of *Lord Althorp*, 1851.
General rules for Commanders, Officers and Chief Engineers, 1889.
Volume of crew lists, 1938.
Correspondence re: Merchant Navy Officers Pension Fund, 1939-1961.
Mere Hall, Wirral, Indian Seamen's Home, accounts, plans, correspondence,
photographs, etc.

Fleet

Specifications for building steel and iron sailing ships, 1884 and 1885.
Hull specification, single-screw steamer, 1898.
Specification for steel twin-screw cargo steamer, 1911.
Agreement for construction and sale of steamships, 1913, 1914, 1915, 1916,
1917, 1919, 1924, 1925, 1937, 1939.
Legal protests re: damage or loss to vessels, 1939-1940, 1955.
Folder, values of ships, 1921-1935.
Log of *Princess Charlotte*, 1826.
Log of *Ariel*, 1831.

Log of *Boyton*, 1841.

Whitehaven Shipbuilding

Dimensions of ships built and repaired, 1792-1841.
Shipyard ledgers, 1818-1865.
Shipyard journals, 1832-1865.
Original plans of ships built at the yard, 1792 (*Nestor*) – 1863 (*Everest*)

World Wars I and II

Files relating to losses, experiences of staff, awards for gallantry, etc.
Reminiscences of sea staff of World War I.
Record of decorations and recommendations, 1939-1945.
Official protests against torpedoing of Brocklebank vessels, 1939-1945.
Radio logs of ships, 1944-1945.
Confidential logs, 1941-1945.
Ms. memoir *T. & J. Brocklebank and the Great War* by A.R. Hughes.
Log of MV *Samovar* towing MV *Trocas*, 1943.
Folder containing application for trading licence, 1948, certificate for government tonnage replacement scheme, 1941; agreement with Ministry of Shipping, 1940; correspondence re: wartime dock labour, 1941 and fire prevention, 1942-1943.

Photographs

Series of ship photographs – *Tenasserim* (1861), *Mahout II* (1936) – five boxes (listed).
Four further boxes containing four albums of miscellaneous vessels, set of photographic copies of paintings from *Swallow* (1805) to *Pindari* (1891), some undated, miscellaneous loose photographs.

Historical Notes (mostly compiled by W.S. Rees)

Notes on fleet, 1770-1962.
Notes of voyage details, 1770-1901.
Notes on Calcutta trade, 1814-1933.
Sailings to China, 1829-1911.
Sailings to Bombay, 1833-1885.
Marine Superintendents in Liverpool, 1836-1934.
Notes on building specifications, launches, report of fast passages, 1834-1858.

Brocklebank Family

Copies of parish register entries, 1734-1779.

Epitome of will of Thomas Brocklebank, 1843.

Licence of Thomas Fisher to take the name of Brocklebank, 1845; official appointments of Thomas Brocklebank, 1864 and 1869; papers re: baronetcy, 1885.

Obituary volume of Sir Aubrey Brocklebank, 1929.

Miscellaneous

Illustrated diary of voyage by W. Alleyn on Tenasserim & Majestic to India, 1882-1883.

B/BROC	(1734)- Brock.family notes, not firm's Archives. 1775-c.1970	105 Boxes

Reference

Gibson, J.F. *Brocklebanks*. Liverpool, 1953.

Canadian Pacific

The Canadian Pacific Railway Co. (CPR) entered the steamship business in 1883 when it bought three ships to operate on the Great Lakes and to assist in building the trans-Canada railway, completed in 1887. The first of the "Empress" ships was ordered in 1889 to run between Vancouver and Yokohama and Hong Kong. In 1903 the company strengthened its Atlantic links, aiming to provide a complete cargo and passenger service from Liverpool to Asia by the purchase of the fourteen ships of the Beaver Line from Elder Dempster. In 1904 two large 14,000-ton "Empress" liners were ordered. On 18 May 1914 the *Empress of Ireland* collided and sank in the St. Lawrence with the loss of over 1000 lives. In 1915 the Allan Line was taken over. In 1922 the whole fleet was reorganised as Canadian Pacific Steamships Ltd. and the following year the express service was moved from Liverpool to Southampton. The fleet carried a million tons of cargo and a million troops and civilians in the Second World War. In 1952 *Empress of Canada* burned in Gladstone Dock, Liverpool. By the 1960s air traffic cut deeply into North Atlantic passenger trade and cruise operations were increased to compensate. CPR's ocean passenger services ended on 23 November 1971 with the docking at Liverpool of *Empress of Canada III*.

The museum has models of *Empress of France* (1928) and *Empress of Britain* (1931).

Records

Hall family: personal papers of D.B. Hall Senior and Junior, Captain R.M. Hall, including cargo stowage books and correspondence.
DX/1120   1925-1980   2 Boxes

P. Spilsbury, Assistant Cruise Director, c. 1930-1940, including large collection of cruise brochures, "Empress" brochures and voyage ephemera.
D/SPI   1883-1968   4 Boxes

Captain G.C. Evans, OBE, senior commander of Canadian Pacific Railway Line, also of Brocklebank and Beaver Line. Played a significant role in World War I; also helped in transferring 4500 Doukhobours from the Black Sea to Canada on *Lake Huron*, 1898. Papers include personal logs, list of deaths of 1898 on *Lake Huron*.
D/EV   1881-1923   3 Boxes
Also DX/SAS series

Reference

Musk, G. *Canadian Pacific*. Newton Abbot, 1981.

China Mutual Steam Navigation Co.

Set up in 1882 with backing from Manchester merchants, the China Mutual was intended to fight the Far East Conference's control of freight rates and Ocean Steam Ship Co.'s near monopoly of the export of Lancashire and Yorkshire textiles. After a fierce rate war waged in partnership with the Mogul Line between 1887 and 1891, it was obliged to join the new Homeward Conference in 1891 and the Outward in 1894. It was taken over by Ocean in 1902. Its records are wholly integrated into the Ocean Steam Ship Co. Archives. The museum also has a half-model of its steamer, *Oopack*, 1883.

Records

Board agendas/brief minutes, 1900-1902.
Articles of association, 1882.
Directors, meeting and ordinary general meetings, 1883-1889.
Prospectus, 1882.
Investment papers, 1903-1911, 1941.
Registers of members, 1892-1918.
Ledgers, 1898-1902.
Ships, account ledger, 1895.

Captain's commissions, depreciation statements, 1910-1957.
Voyage book, 1900-1902.
Dock officers' and engineers' records, 1895-1902.
Steamer earnings, 1902-1968.
Reports of sinkings, 1915-1918.
OA   1882-1968

Reference

Falkus, M. *The Blue Funnel Legend. A History of the Ocean Steam Ship Co.,
    1865-1971.* London, 1990.

Clan Line

Charles Cayzer, a Liverpool shipbroker, started a Liverpool and Glasgow to
Bombay cargo line with six steamers in 1878. Within four years the Clan Line
had successfully expanded to make calls at other Indian ports and started a South
African service. East African and Red Sea destinations were added in 1880. It
lost twenty-eight ships in the First World War and twenty-seven in the Second;
but it remained one of the largest Liverpool-based cargo liner fleets into the
early 1960s. In 1959 it became part of the British and Commonwealth Shipping
Group and by 1981 it had sold its last ship. The company Archives are deposited
at the National Maritime Museum. This museum holds models of *Clan MacNeil*
(1891) and *Clan MacDonald* (turret steamer, 1897), slides of the passage of a
Clan liner up the Manchester Ship Canal in 1974.

Records

Manuscript diary of a young girl, Isa Foster Barham, who left Liverpool for
    Bombay on 3 November 1894, aboard *Clan Macintosh*, which suffered
    a broken shaft and was towed into Aden for repair. The girl and her
    family eventually reached Bombay on another vessel. 3 Nov. 1894-22
    April 1895.
DX/652

Brochure for the passenger service to Colombo, Madras and Calcutta, c. 1950.
SAS/29/3/15

Reference

Middlemiss, H.L. *Gathering of the Clans. History of Clan Line Steamers Ltd.*
    Newcastle-upon-Tyne, 1988.

Coast Lines Ltd.

Coast Lines of Liverpool was formed by the merger of three coastal passenger and cargo lines (Powell, Bacon and Hough) in 1913. The Coast Lines title was adopted in 1917 when the group was taken into the Royal Mail Group. After the dissolution of the latter in 1931 Coast Lines remained independent until its takeover by P&O in 1971. Under the chairmanship of Sir Alfred Read (see MDHB/WUP/LA) it acquired some twenty coasting companies including W.A. Savage's Zillah Shipping Co. in 1949 (see separate entry). Coast Lines ran cargo liner services to all major British ports and dominated Irish sea passenger services. Its Archives are at the National Maritime Museum. The MDHB collection contains substantial evidence of its Liverpool operation which took up most of the berths from Princes to Bramley Moore dock. The museum holds a large number of models of Coast Lines' and their subsidiary companies' ships from the *Somerset Coast* (ex-*Graceful*) 1911, to the *Ulster Queen*, 1967, together with paintings, including a portrait of Sir Alfred Read.

Records

Publicity material.
SAS/33A/1/6
Map showing Coast Lines sailing routes of Great Britain.
SAS/33A/1/7
Articles of partnership, agreements, etc., relating to Powell and Hough, 1890,
      Alsop Wilkinson solicitors collection.
B/AW/67
Log Lines, the Coast Lines house journal, various issues, 1946-1968.
Library (see volume 2).
Unpublished biography of Sir Alfred Read by J. Winter-Lotimer, 1986.
Library (see volume 2).

Reference

Reader, E.R. *The World's Largest Coastwise Liner Fleet*. Liverpool, 1949.

William Cory and Son Ltd.

The actual date of the first establishment of the firm in the coal business is unknown but it was certainly before 1785. The first William Cory definitely associated with the firm was living near Lambeth Wharf in 1811. In 1838 the firm took the name William Cory and Son. Up to the 1850s, apart from barges and lighters, Cory chartered more ships than it owned. At a time when most coal was carried in sail it took shares in one of the pioneer steam colliers in

1854. In 1861 it had a floating pontoon built, equipped with hydraulic cranes to speed up coal discharge. By the 1870s it handled half the London coal trade.

In 1896 when the records begin Cory amalgamated with seven other companies connected with coal and the distinctive colour scheme, a black diamond, was chosen for all the ships concerned. The records of one of these firms, Thames Steam and Lighterage Co. Ltd., go back to 1857. The combined fleet was insufficient for the trade and ships of other companies were constantly taken on time charter. By the outbreak of war in 1914 the company had twenty-seven colliers. Despite the priority given to warship building, Cory managed to obtain new tonnage during the war. In World War II, out of regard for the importance of coal, the company was allowed to build several ships. During the war Cory was called upon to manage a number of foreign ships for the Ministry of War Transport. It also established a French subsidiary. During World War II one of the Directors, Lord Leathers, was Minister of War Transport.

The company became one of the best-known bunkering firms with depots all over the globe for coal and/or oil and, through its subsidiaries, was engaged in shipbuilding, agency work, lighterage, towage and salvage, wharfage, sand and ballast, warehousing, cold storage, road haulage, shipping and forwarding, air freight, export packing and travel. It finished with colliers in the 1970s but is still one of the biggest tug owners. Cory was taken over by Ocean Transport and Trading in 1972, and its Archives was completely integrated with that of the new parent company. The museum also holds the important model of the floating pontoon, *Atlas 1* (1858).

Records

Secretarial

Board minutes, 1896-1972; minutes of Cory Tank Craft Ltd., 1900-1953; Cory
    Colliers Ltd., 1916-1957; Cory Lighterage Ltd., 1916-1952; Cory
    Mann George Ltd., 1917-1966; Cory and Strick Ltd., 1927-1962; Cory
    Stowage and Distribution Services, 1947-1960; Cory Sand and Ballast,
    1948-1956, Societe Francaise, Wm. Cory et Fils, 1916-1952; Wharfage
    and Lighterage Division, 1963-1966; McGregor Cory (Europe) Ltd.,
    1930-1957; Subsidiary companies include Thomas Steam Tug and
    Lighterage Co. Ltd., 1857-1962; Association Ltd., R. and J.H. Rea
    Ltd. Board minutes, 1901-1927, 1941-1966; Steamship Owners Coal
    Association, 1899-1964 (over thirty other companies involved in coal
    and allied distribution).
Articles of association, various companies, 1859-1919.
Prospectus re: amalgamation, 1896.
Agreements and letters, 1919-1925.
Seal books, 1896-1969.

James W. Cook and Co. (Wivenhoe) Ltd., shipbuilders, seal and agenda books, 1948-1963.
Bills of sale, 1900-1965.
Investment, director and shareholders records, 1900-1963.
Management council, reports to Board, 1936-1963.
Letterbook, Weber Smith and Hoard (Overseas) Ltd., 1926-1930.
Staff pension scheme minute book, 1921-1967.

Management

Engineering report to Management Council, 1936-1949, 1957-1963.

Staff

Engineer offices service record books, c. 1900 - c. 1950.

Fleet

List of Cory ships, 1839 onwards.
Register of Thames and Medway Tugs and Barge fleets, 1950, 1952 and 1964.
Register of Barges, 1936.

Publicity

Press cuttings, 1944-c. 1977; advertisements, 1943-1955.
Photographs of tugs, wharves, buildings, etc.

House Magazines

Black Diamond, 1922-1929.
Cory News, 1971-1972.

Unofficial Records

A number of books, articles and papers, published and unpublished, relevant to company history.
OA   1857-1972   (see Ocean Steam Ship Co.)

Reference

Johnston, C.H. "'Black Diamonds' by Sea," *Sea Breezes*, New series, X (1950), 268-283.

Cunard Line

In 1838 the British government, impressed by the advantages of steam over sail for making regular passages, invited tenders to carry the transatlantic mails by steamer. The contract, which carried a subsidy, was won by Samuel Cunard, a prominent merchant and shipowner of Halifax, Nova Scotia, and an advocate of steam. With the help of Robert Napier, the Clyde shipbuilder, and his partners George Burns and David McIver, who already owned a coastal steamer business, he set up the British and North American Royal Mail Steam Packet Co. The service started with four wooden paddle steamers in 1840. In 1847 the service was increased to a weekly sailing in each direction. In 1852 the firm introduced screw-propelled ships on its Mediterranean service but, with its emphasis on reliability and safety, retained paddlers for its main service until the mid-1860s. By this decade iron hulls became standard too. It was also a period of reduced subsidies and increased competition from lines such as Inman, National and White Star. In 1878 it was reinvigorated as the Cunard Steam Ship Co. Ltd. and the fleet modernised. The 14,000-ton twin-screw liners, *Campania* and *Lucania* (1893) were milestones in terms of both size and speed. But by 1902 with the formation of the American combine, the International Mercantile Marine, and German competition it was under threat. In 1904 it took the bold step of building the steam turbine-powered 20,000-ton *Carmania*. Its success led to the building (with government assistance) of two 32,000-ton express liners, *Mauretania* and *Lusitania* (1907) which captured the Blue Riband.

The line had contributed to naval campaigns from the Crimean War onwards and in the First World War it lost thirteen of its twenty-six ships, including *Lusitania*, which was torpedoed in 1915 (see volume 2). *Carmania* fought a notable action as an armed merchant cruiser and other vessels were used as transports, hospital ships, armed cruisers and a seaplane carrier.

After the war the fleet was rebuilt and included the ex-German liner *Berengaria* (formerly *Imperator*). The express service was moved from Liverpool to Southampton in 1919 and eventually two large liners, *Queen Mary* (1936) and *Queen Elizabeth* (1940) were built with government help. Both played vital roles as troopships in the Second World War. The White Star Line was acquired in 1934.

The line prospered after the war but passenger traffic declined in the 1960s, leading to a change from regular transatlantic services to cruising only, and to entry into the Atlantic Container Lines consortium for cargo services in 1966. In 1971 it was taken over by Trafalgar House Investments Ltd. which continue to own cruise ships, including *Queen Elizabeth 2* (1969) and the container ship, *Atlantic Conveyor* (a replacement for the ship of the same name sunk in the Falklands War in 1982). The rest of the cargo shipping (Cunard-Brocklebank) was merged with Ellerman's remaining shipping interests and sold to Andrew Weir Shipping in 1991. Cunard owned a number of important subsidiaries. Anchor, Brocklebank and White Star are described under their own sections.

The museum's holdings consist mainly of plans and records from the naval architect's offices and a rich collection of printed ephemera in the SAS and DX miscellaneous collections including menus, postcards and souvenir brochures. There is a fine collection of models including a twenty-foot model of *Berengaria*, paintings, uniforms and other relics. Administrative records, including passenger lists (1840-1853) and records of the Port Line, are held by Liverpool University Archives; its catalogue is in the museum's reading room.

Records

Naval Architect's Department

Technical Committee minutes, 1921-1927, 1937 (fragile).
Supporting papers, 1927-1930.
Miscellaneous papers, 1916-1963.
Correspondence files, 1914-1916, 1935-1959; letterbooks, 1935-1959.
Instruction book, 1911-1939; Black list book, 1929-1935.
Newscuttings books, 1919-1938.
Box files on new steamers, c. 1920-c. 1930.
Sets of Cunard general arrangements for c. fifteen liners including *Mauretania 1* and *Queen Mary*.
Ships' plans, approximately ninety vessels, 1840-c. 1970 (note: the drawings of some of the earlier vessels are fragile).
Naval Architect's log data books, 1919-1920 (four vessels).
Ships' specifications, 1898-1962.

Marine Engineer's Department

General Abstracts of logs, 1858-1897.
Abstracts of logs, particular vessels, 1893-1930.
Voyage data books, 1874-1886, 1904-1933 (Atlantic), 1932-1949 (general).
Coal consumption, 1907-1913.
Oil consumption, 1908-1931.

Additional Material

Articles of association, 1912.
Reports and accounts, 1954-1969.
Embarkation notices, 1963.
Ephemera, 1960-1965.
Brochures, 1908-1939.

Postcards, including sinking of *Campania* (1918).
Photographs, a large collection including some very large and fine interiors, some by Bedford Le Mere, c. 1910-1970.
Volume of certificates of British Registry of Cunard vessels, 1936-1966.
Brochures on opening of Cunard offices, Pier Head, c. 1919.
Freight rate schedules, 1878-1921.
Atlantic Container Line timetable, 1988.
B/CUN 1840-1988 ninety-three boxes, c. fifty vols., c. fifty rolls of plans

Ephemera and Stray Material

There is also much in the SAS and DX series. Because of the Bates connection, there is Cunard ephemera in the Brocklebank Archives, and some Brocklebank ships' specifications (1918-1958) in the Cunard material. Of particular interest in the SAS series are verbatim reports of general meetings, 1882-1889.

Reference

Hyde, F.E. *Cunard and the North Atlantic 1840-1973*. London, 1975.

Dominion Line

This company, as the Liverpool and Mississippi Steamship Co., was formed in 1870 to capitalise on the increase of trade with the southern states after the end of the American Civil War. It expanded its services to include Quebec and Montreal in 1872, changing its name to the Mississippi and Dominion Steamship Co., abbreviated to Dominion Line. Emigrants to Canada comprised the bulk of its weekly service to Quebec and Montreal, calling at Irish ports en route. The company was bought by IMM in 1902 and from 1909 until 1926 the Canadian trade was maintained as a joint service with White Star.

     The museum holds models of *Vancouver*, 1884, and *Mayflower*, 1902, (ex-*Hanoverian*, later *Cretic* and *Devonian*).

Records

Papers relating to Henry Eves, life-saving medal and certificate presented on board SS *Ottoman* for rescuing crew from the Dutch schooner *Anna*, including a letter from Dominion Lines re: the incident.
SAS/23A/2/15

Advertisement for Dominion Line sailings, c. 1875-1880.
SAS/SSF/3/1

Reference

Bonsor, N.R.P. *North Atlantic Seaway. Vol. 2.* Jersey, 1979, 787-813.

Elder Dempster and Co. (and successors)

In 1868 John Dempster went into partnership with John Elder, the brother of the eminent Glasgow shipbuilder, Alexander, to act as Liverpool agents of the British and African Steam Navigation Co. of Glasgow. The company's vessels were constructed in John Elder's Fairfield (Glasgow) yard. The British and African and the older African Steam Ship Co., both with headquarters in Liverpool, prospered and came to an arrangement to divide sailings. In 1875 Alfred Lewis Jones (later Sir Alfred Jones) set up a shipping and insurance broking office in Liverpool under the name Alfred L. Jones and Co., and with some small chartered sailing vessels began trading with West Africa. By 1879 Jones, whose competition was feared, was made a junior partner in Elder Dempster. By 1884, he was left as the controlling partner of Elder Dempster and by 1890 he had bought a controlling interest in the African Steam Ship Co.

In 1884 Alfred Jones introduced the banana to England. From 1890 he energetically expanded his business with new transatlantic sailings, the purchase of the Beaver Line in 1898 (re-sold 1903), supplying transport for the Boer War, setting up the Imperial Direct Line from Avonmouth to Jamaica, and taking over the British and African Steam Navigation Co. in 1900. On his death in 1909 Elder Dempster and its 109 ships were bought by Sir Owen Philipp's (later Lord Kylsant) Royal Mail Group. The new owners faced considerable competition in the West African trade, notably from Lever Brothers and John Holt and Co. The firm also suffered the loss of forty-two vessels in the First World War and postwar trading to West Africa remained competitive and problematic (especially in the relationship with the United Africa Co). The overall position of the Royal Mail Group deteriorated rapidly after 1929, leading to collapse in 1932. A new Elder Dempster Line was reconstructed under the management of the Ocean Steam Ship Co. Ltd. Recovery was cut short by the Second World War in which forty-one ships were sunk. After the war trade increased, the fleet was modernised, and other lines acquired including the Henderson Line in 1953 (see separate entry), Guinea Gulf (see John Holt entry) in 1965, and Palm Line in 1985. In 1965 Liner Holdings Co., which held the Elder Dempster vessels, was incorporated into Ocean, hence the inclusion of its records within the Ocean Archives. Trade to West Africa became increasingly difficult for many reasons including the rise of national shipping companies and the political situation. By 1989 Elder Dempster had sold its ships and was itself sold by Ocean Transport and Trading.

The records have the same problem as the Ocean Archives (see Ocean entry). The museum also holds a number of ship models including *Ethiope* (1854), *Winnebar* (ex-*Umtata*, 1935), *Aureol* (1951) and *Maron* (1980).

Records

Secretarial

General meeting minutes, 1932-1964.
Directors minutes, 1932-1973.
Management Committee minutes, 1947-1968.

Financial

Accounts, 1942-c. 1980.
West African Lighterage and Transport Ltd. annual returns, 1931-1954; journal, 1953-1960.
Kroo labour accounts, 1962-1963.
Liverpool Dock Organisation, returns of accounts ledger, 1958-1959.

Legal and Administrative

Trade agreements, articles of association of subsidiary and associated companies, 1891-1960.
Miscellaneous contracts, 1948-1954.

Management

Papers of partners and senior managers, 1934-1977, inc. M.B. Glasier, CBE.

Other Papers

Files re: reconstruction of company after Royal Mail crisis, 1935-1938.
Integration with Ocean Steam Ship Co., 1965.
Nigerian Lighterage Co., feasibility study 1976.
Various reports and studies, 1960-1980.
Correspondence re: Nigerian Union of Seamen, 1955-1962.
Nigerian Shipping Federation, 1960-1968.
Accra anchorages and deep draught ships, 1955.
Guinea Gulf Lines, 1964-1968.

Staff

Salary scales, 1954-1966.
Registers of officers (broken series), 1897-1958.
Registers of engineers, 1920-1947.
Doctor's record book, 1946-1968.
Instructions and notices to engineers, etc., 1970s.
Steamer itinerary showing captains, pursers and doctors on vessels, 1919-1926.
Training and recruitment papers, c. 1965.

Cargo Records

Conference and trade enforcements, UK/West Africa, 1924-1962; Henderson
    Line re: Burma, 1970.
Early West Africa letters, 1871-1953.
Misc agreements of instructions, 1960-1970.
Storage plans, MV *Eboe*, 1952-1977; MV *Dumbaia*, 1960.
Sample bills of lading, 1951.
Sample cargo notes, 1955 and 1968.
Cargo tally book, 1947.
Capacity plans, c. 1960-1970.
Running costs, 1958-1967.
Intermediate freight lists, 1958-1967.
Freight tariff notes, 1957.

Passenger Records

RMS *Hilary*, time charter party, 1956 (chartered from Booth Line).
Accident file, 1956.
Numerous accommodation plans, brochures, etc., c. 1900-1960.
Ephemeral passenger lists, 1909 and 1948.
Pursers' accounts, 1947-1962.
Berthing Lists, 1973-1974.

Fleet Records

Fleet lists, 1852-1966.
Fleet Books, 1960-1970.
Some ships' plans, twentieth century.
World War II records, coastal craft record, 1934-1945.
Naval Architect's data books, 1901-1958.
Contracts, 1952-1962.
Ship survey records, 1934-1952.

Eboe launch ephemera, 1951.
Ephemera, e.g., diaries, calendars, 1940-1974.
Various posters and films including *Aureol* voyage, 1969, 1950-1970.

Photographs

Extensive collection of all kinds, both negatives and prints, c. 1895-1976.

House Magazines

Elder Dempster Magazine, 1922-1926.
Sea House Magazine, 1953-1976 (articles indexed).
Elders of Elders Pensioners Newsletter, 1971 on.

Airline Records

Papers re: Imperial Airways, 1935.
Nigeria Airways, 1958-1961.

Miscellaneous Records

Reminiscences of T.A. Porter, c. 1898; H. Cotterell, 1863-1910; report of M.
        Warriner, 1892-1909.
OA   1871-1970   (See Ocean Steam Ship Co. Ltd.)

References

Davies, P.N. *The Trade Makers. Elder Dempster in West Africa, 1852-1972.*
        London, 1973.

Cowden, J.E. and Duffy, J.O.C. *The Elder Dempster Fleet History, 1852-1985.*
        Norwich, 1986.

Ellerman Lines

John Ellerman was an accountant, son of a Hamburg merchant who settled in
Hull. The Liverpool and London shipowner, Frederick Leyland, who had bought
the Bibby Line (and renamed it after himself) in 1873, died suddenly in 1892.
Ellerman (barely thirty) with Christopher Furness and Henry O'Hagan, bought
Frederick Leyland and Co. Within a year Ellerman had succeeded Christopher
Furness as chairman and managing director. In 1900 he took over the Liverpool
firm, West India and Pacific Steamship Co. In 1901 Ellerman sold his fleet to
J. Pierpont Morgan, the American financier, whose aim was to establish a

worldwide shipping combine, the International Mercantile Marine. Ellerman arranged to buy back the ships serving the Mediterranean, Portugal, Montreal and Antwerp. He augmented his new fleet by the purchase of the Papayanni City and Hall Lines in 1901. These formed a new company, Ellerman Lines Ltd. Westcott and Laurance, which traded from London to the Mediterranean, was purchased in 1902 and Bucknall trading to South Africa in 1908.

The larger of the purchased lines remained distinct units after their acquisition. In 1916 the Wilson Line of Hull (with sixty-seven short-sea vessels) was purchased by Ellerman personally. The group lost ships in the First World War and weathered the financial crises of the interwar period. Ellerman died a baronet with a fortune of £37 million in 1933. By 1939 the group owned 109 ships of 919,969 dwt., of which fifty-eight were lost in the Second World War. The ships were replaced but trading became more difficult with newly independent nations, such as India, setting up their own shipping companies, and the introduction of containerisation.

In 1966 Ellerman joined the Associated Container Lines consortium and started the successful containerisation of the Mediterranean services. In 1973 the group, which by now had many other interests beyond shipping including hotels, brewing and printing, merged all its shipping companies into one division. Ten years later the whole business was sold to the Barclay brothers after making heavy losses. In 1985 the shipping business was purchased by its management, then sold to Trafalgar House to become Cunard-Ellerman in 1987 and finally in 1991 it passed to the Andrew Weir Shipping Group.

The component lines, Hall, Papayanni and ACT, have their own entries. The University of Glasgow holds a major Ellerman Archives which is strong on the City Line but has material relating to the whole group as well. A copy of this list is available in the reading room. The museum also holds a superb model of *City of Manchester*, 1950.

Records

Finance

Ledgers (agents, voyage), 1903-1937; (disbursements, clearing, private), 1966-1968.

Operational

Particulars of steamers, 1934.
Particulars of fleet, 1966.
Trim and stability books, 1956, 1968.
Freight manifests, 1971.
Passenger record book, 1949-1972.

Staff

Reference books, masters and mates, 1918-1962.

Miscellaneous

Newscuttings book, 1964-1970.
B/ELP   1903 - 1972   11 Boxes and 8 Volumes

Ellerman City Liners

Ephemera and publicity material, 1984-1987.
World map showing Ellerman's shipping routes (1 Box).

Miscellaneous Companies

Minutes of Douro Steamship Co., 1880-1888.
Combined minutes of Asia, Minor, Bear, Bravo, Esperanza and Milo Steamship
        Cos., 1906-1917.
Registers of shareholders of: Netherby Steamship Co., 1890-1898; Leyden
        Steamship Co., 1897-1898.
Register of Returns for Bravo, 1906-1912; Esperanza and Milo Steamship Cos.
Papers relating to affairs of C. and H. Crichton and CBS Engineering, Ship
        repairers.
Balance sheets, 1922-1926.
Other records, 1936-1972.
Volume of freight manifests, Coverley, 1958-1965; Westray, Walbaum, Tosetti,
        London
B/ELM   1880-1972   4 Boxes and 1 Volume

Ellerman Line Ltd.

(Acquired from J. Bryson, via Liverpool University)
Cash books of J.R. Ellerman, 1903-1904.
General cash books, Ellerman Lines Ltd., 1907-1930.
DB/EL   1904-1930   14 Volumes

Reference

Haws, D. *Ellerman Lines* Hereford, 1989.

Taylor, J. *Ellermans. A Wealth of Shipping*. London, 1976.

Furness, Withy and Co.

Christopher Furness' shipping company developed from his family's wholesale grocery import business at West Hartlepool. Initially in partnership with his brother, he set up his own shipowning company in 1881 and in 1883 was joined by Edward Withy, owner of a local shipyard. Furness, Withy and Co. (incorporated in 1893) expanded to run a service from London to North America, as well as buying interests in a steelworks, collieries and insurance. From 1898 it acquired Manchester Liners, the first of many shipping company purchases, which later included the Warren Line (1911), Johnston and Prince Lines (1916), Cairn Line (1928), Bowring and Co. (1929), Shaw, Savill and Albion (1934) and the Royal Mail Line and the Pacific Steam Navigation Co. (1965). After the loss of thirty-six ships in the First World War, the company was bought by its managers in 1919 and proceeded to rebuild its fleet at the Furness shipyard. Vessels included six new motor vessels for a European-West Coast of North America service in 1922 and luxury cruises from New York to the West Indies in 1927. By the outbreak of the Second World War, the company was running ships to all parts of the world. It remained a major force in British shipping despite the loss of forty-six vessels in the war. As with the other major British groups, it tried to keep pace with rapidly changing conditions in the 1960s; it was a partner in Overseas Containers; it containerised the Manchester-Canada service and much of the South American trade; while its Houlder subsidiary successfully diversified into the offshore oil business. In 1980 Furness, Withy (Shipping) Ltd. was taken over by the Hong Kong shipowner, C.Y. Tung, and in 1990 was sold to Hamburg-Sud A.G., which run container services from northern Europe and the Mediterranean to South America and New Zealand as well as a round-the-world service. All the records are part of the PSNC Archives.

Records

Furness Withy Liverpool salaries volume, 1921-1924.
Pension scheme papers, 1974-1980.
Finance and Accounts, 1965-1978.
Employee's handbook, 1980.
Sea Staff Newsletters, 1981-1982.
Papers re: Art Award Scheme, 1978-1980.
Career and publicity ephemera, 1960-1978.
PSNC   1921-1978   (see PSNC)

Reference

Middlemiss, N.L. *Furness-Houlder Lines*. Newcastle-upon-Tyne, 1991.

The Glen and Shire Line

The Ocean Steamship Co. encountered strong competition from the Glen Line, founded by James McGregor, partner in McGregor, Gow and Holland, in 1869 and in the Shire Line, founded by David Jenkins in 1861. The latter had originally been a sailing fleet which changed to steam in 1872. Jenkins was among the first to perceive the great economic potential of Japan, with which he traded more than with China, and he helped to establish the Japanese shipping line, NYK.

The first Glen steamers were built primarily for the China tea trade. Towards the end of the century increased competition in that trade and the development of tea-growing in India and Ceylon caused a heavy fall in freights. Nevertheless, in 1895 the line was maintaining fortnightly sailings from London to the Far East and making average passage to Hong Kong in forty days.

The Shire Line went through a difficult period culminating in the Russo-Japanese war, as a result of which it sold a half share to T. & J. Brocklebank in 1906. In 1907 Royal Mail, under Sir Owen Philipps, bought a sixth share from Brocklebank and another sixth from the Shire Line and so obtained a third share. In 1910 Glen Line was acquired by Elder Dempster, which Royal Mail had bought in 1909. Glen and Shire were sister lines, running co-ordinated but separate services.

The Glen Line was a pioneer of motor ships and improved cargo gear in the 1920s. It was also in financial difficulties and did not pay a dividend after 1923. The Kylsant Group's collapse led to its sale to Ocean and integration in 1935. Glen continued to operate from London, but the development of container services (especially Ocean's participation in OCL from 1965) led in 1974 to a combined conventional service with Blue Funnel, its Dutch subsidiary and Ben Line (Ben Ocean), which gradually dwindled by 1986.

The records contain very little Shire Line material. The problems of the Ocean Archives cataloguing system also apply to the Glen Line records. The museum holds a fine model of *Glenlyon* (1962).

Records

Secretarial

Management Committee minutes, 1924-1935.
Board of Directors minutes, McGregor, Gow and Holland, 1912-1936.
Annual Meeting minutes, 1911-1974.
Directors' Meetings and balance sheets, 1930-1965.
Directors' attendance books, 1912-1966.
Articles of association, 1912.
Shire Line Agreements, 1907-1933 (some signed by Owen Philipps).
Papers re: Royal Mail Shipping Group affairs (Kylsant Crash), 1931-1935.
Register of Directors' interests, 1937-1956.
Share Book, McGregor, Gow, Norris and Joyner, 1902-1965.
List of shareholders and directors, McGregor, Gow and Holland, 1918-1939.
Register of shareholders, Glen Line, 1910-1970.
Correspondence re: merger with Ocean Steamship Co., 1935.

Financial

Share accounts on ships, 1871.
Private ledger, McGregor, Gow, Norris and Joyner, 1912-1947.
Voyage results, 1935-1949.

Management

Personal files relating to leading personalities in the firm's management, including Sir Stewart McTier, Sir Herbert McDavid, W.A. McNeile, 1913-1969.

Correspondence

Mostly re: World War II matters and de-requisition, 1964-1969.

Staff

Office staff salary book, 1912-1916.
Deck officers service records, 1927; registers, c. 1950-1960.
Engineers records of service, etc., 1890-1982.
Stewards' records, 1914-1957.
Chinese crews, various papers re: labour relations, etc., 1967-1969.
Seamen's strike, 1961.
Wages books, 1935-1965.

Operational instructions, 1947-1967.

Cargo

Booking list, 1939-1940.
Miscellaneous documents, including bills of lading, c. 1940-c. 1960.
Ministry of Transport letters, World War II.
Steamer earnings, 1871-1898.
Freight movements, 1901-1919.
Homeward earnings and prize freights, World War II.
Voyage accounts, 1970-1975.

Passengers

Sailing cards, 1911-1970.
Fare schedules, 1935-1974.

Trade, General

Suez Canal correspondence, 1953-1964.

Fleet

Ships journals, 1881-1945.
Steamer tonnages, 1883-1916.
Records re: World War II operations.
Stowage factors by ships, 1946-c. 1960.
Shipwrights data books, 1913-1950.
Other records including drawings, specifications and contracts.
Press reports, 1936, 1950-1968.
Press cuttings, 1876-1950.
Publicity material and ephemera, 1879-1969, including sailing cards, albums,
          notices.
Papers relating to company property, Hull and overseas, 1928-1934.

Photographs

Ships, personalities, port scenes, events, 1871-1966.

Unofficial Records

Number of books, articles and papers relevant to company history.
OA   1871-1975   (see Ocean Steam Ship Co. Ltd.)

Reference

Falkus, M. *The Blue Funnel Legend. A History of the Ocean Steamship Co., 1865-1971*. London, 1990.

Guion Line

Stephen Guion, part-owner of the New York-Liverpool Old Black Star Line of sailing packets and manager of Cunard's emigrant business (1862-1866), set up his own steamship line, Liverpool and Great Western Steamship Co. or Guion Line, in 1866. It had a successful start and by 1870 had six ships; a seventh *Wisconsin* was the first compound-engined steamer on the Atlantic. Innovation continued with water-tube boilers on *Dakota* and *Montana* in 1872 – not a success – and the record-breaking *Arizona* of 1879, *Alaska* of 1881 and *Oregon* of 1884. Guion's death in 1885, poor traffic and the high cost of its big fast ships led to decline and winding up in 1894.

The museum holds a painting and model of *Abyssinia* (1870), bought from Cunard in 1881, and relics from the wreck of *Dakota* (1877).

Records

Guidebook, Liverpool, London, Paris, 1875.
SAS/33/F/3/3

Ticket for passage to New York on *Arizona*, 1892.
B/AW/22

Poster, c. 1890
DX/596

Plan of *Oregon*, 1882, Cunard collection.

Reference

Bonsor, N.R.P. *North Atlantic Seaway. Vol. 2*. Jersey, 1979, 701-711.

Hall Line

The Hall Line originated as Sun Shipping Co. founded by Robert Alexander, a Belfast-born but Liverpool-based shipbroker, in 1868. It concentrated on the Indian trade with Bombay as its main port. Alexander's ships were re-organised from two groups into the Hall Line in 1899 and sold to Ellerman in 1901. Under Ellerman's ownership it developed successful South and East African services as well as holding its own in the competitive Indian trade. It suffered from disruption and loss of ships in both World Wars and from the granting of Indian independence and the establishment of Indian national lines. In 1973 it merged with the other Ellerman shipping companies to form Ellerman City Liners.

Records

Administration

Directors' minute books, 1899-1934, 1956-1967.
Agenda book, 1899-1901.
Registers, 1899, 1901, 1968, 1971.
Letterbooks, 1885-1911, 1964.
Seal books, 1899-1971.
Annual returns books, 1930-1962.
Notices for general meetings, 1906-1910, 1919.

Legal

Memoranda and articles of association, 1899, 1949, 1950, 1966.
Instruments of protest, 1927-1941.
Large class of miscellaneous legal and operational documents (600+ items)
      numbered but only roughly listed, 1881-1964.
Contracts (for docking, stevedoring), 1888-1895.
Miscellaneous (including indemnities, guarantees, war damage claims),
      1899-1941.

Investment

Annual list and summary, 1875-1898 (Sun Shipping Co. Ltd.).
Annual list and summary, 1899-1929 (Hall Line Ltd.).
Debenture records, 1899-1901.
Transfer records, 1899-1970.
Interest and dividend accounts, etc., 1899-1970.
List of single-ship companies owned, 1910-1911.

Finance

Bank books, 1899.
Balance sheets, 1901-1932, 1950-1962, 1969-1971.
Profit and loss account, 1907-1933.
Annual summary books, 1907-1914, 1919-1935.
Agents' account books, 1945-1967.

Voyage account books, 1966-1967.

Ledgers (including voyage results, general, captains', repair, survey, impersonal, disbursement), 1910-1974.

Journals, day and cash books (including pilots'), 1920-1933, 1942-1947, 1964-1974.

Income tax, 1923-1972.

Port charge books, 1927-1974.

Outward freight adjustments and ledgers, 1966-1968.

Inward freight and charges, 1967.

Insurance

Marine, 1893-1967.

Motor, 1939-1973.

Operational

Movement books, 1900-1969.

Particulars of Steamers, 1919-1934.

Particulars of fleet, 1950, 1970-1971.

Capacity plans book, 1916-1951.

Trim and stability books, 1957-1960.

Casualty reports, 1940-1950.

Miscellaneous (including goods ordered, chartering papers, provisions stockbooks, plans for new engine works), 1899-1973.

Register books for vessels, 1919-1947, 1950-1966.

Book of charter parties, 1935-1956, 1966-1972.

Route agreements, 1875-1956.

Passenger certificates, 1913-1942.

Certificates of survey in dry dock, 1908-1942.

Temporary crew space certificates, 1933-1942.

Staff

Reference books, officers, 1877-1955.

Stewards, 1880-1951.

Carpenters, 1905-1955.

Engineers, 1910-1968.

Record book, apprentices, 1948-1968.

Wages and salary records, 1892-1911, 1955-1973.

Workmen's compensation claims book (natives, stevedores), 1914-1928.

Certificates of competency, 1867-1868.

Sports club, 1951-1970.

Miscellaneous

Private code book, 1938.
B/ELH   1875-c. 1970   c. 140 Boxes and Volumes

Reference

Haws, D. *Ellerman Lines*. Hereford, 1989.

Taylor, J. *Ellermans. A Wealth of Shipping*. London, 1976.

Thos. and Jas. Harrison

Established in 1853, this business grew out of the earlier merchant and shipowning partnership of Brown and Harrison, which specialised in the import of French brandy. In 1857 it bought its first iron sailing ship and in 1860 it bought two steamers which carried brandy to London as well as Liverpool. Competition forced it out of the London trade by 1863; instead the partners successfully started sending sailing ships to India and steamers to Spain and Portugal. These were followed by steam services to New Orleans in 1866 and to India via the Suez Canal in 1869.

The Charente Steamship Co. was set up in 1871 to take on the ownership of the ships with Thos. & Jno. Harrison as managers – a continuing arrangement. The firm continued to prosper and owned twenty-nine ships (all steamers) at the time of James Harrison's death in 1891. They joined the South African Conference in 1902 and this was enhanced by the purchase of John T. Rennie's Aberdeen Direct Line in 1911. At the outbreak of the First World War, Harrison owned over seventy vessels of which twenty-seven were lost. In 1920-1921 it attempted to develop a West Indies business by buying the Crown Line of Glasgow (eight ships) and by transferring three of passenger liners from the South African route. The Great Depression (1929-1933) was a difficult period with fifteen ships laid-up, although a modest upturn followed which led to the acquisition of modern new tonnage and the Gulf of Mexico routes of the defunct Leyland Line. Harrison lost thirty of forty-six ships in the Second World War including the famous "Whisky Galore" *Politician*, wrecked in 1941. The replacements were first, ten Liberty and six Empire-type ships, and then twenty motor ships (Harrison's first), built and engined by Doxford at Sunderland between 1947 and 1955. The berthing rights to the brandy trade were finally sold in the latter year. In 1960 *Adventurer*, with engines aft and a 180-ton Stulcken derrick, was an innovation which was developed in other ships ordered from 1961 to 1972. In 1970 Harrison decided to diversify by buying three bulkers and in 1976 it joined the container consortium, Caribbean Ocean Lines (CAROL) with three ships, in 1978 had a part share with Ellerman in a container ship in the South African European Container Services (SAECS) and in 1981 was a founder of the East African (BEACON) consortium. It also managed bulkers owned by two Hong Kong-registered subsidiaries.

The company maintains its own records at Mersey Chambers, Liverpool. The museum holds two important collections of Harrison Line master's papers, together with pamphlets, newsletters, plans and a model of *Inventor* (1964).

Records

Photocopy of book listing cargo handling equipment, 1895.
DX/SAS/2/916

Captain W.E. Williams collection, c. 1940-1964, including war diaries and
        photographs, stowage plans and notes on navigation.
DX/713

Captain W.L. Ashton collection, 1931-1977, including wage slips, 1931-1941,
        personal voyage book, 1963-1977.
DX/1129

Captain W.L. Ashton's official voyage record book, 1963-1974.
DX/1126

Harrison Line newsletters, 1988-1994.
Ship plans
See MDHB and SAS collections.

Reference

Hyde, F.E. *Harrisons of Liverpool*. Liverpool, 1967.

Haws, D. *Thos. and Jas. Harrison*. Hereford, 1988.

Henderson Line

Founded in 1863 at Glasgow, "Paddy" Henderson's British and Burmese Steam Navigation Co. came to specialise in cargo and passenger services to Burma. It was also closely associated with the Irrawaddy Flotilla Co. (see separate entry). In 1952 it was purchased by Elder Dempster and, as a result, some of its records are incorporated into the Ocean Steam Ship Co. Ltd. collection.

Records

Board minutes, 1874-1935.
Statistics, 1948-1961.
Management correspondence, 1952-1964.
OA   1874   (See Ocean Steam Ship Co. Ltd.)

Reference

Laird, D. *Paddy Henderson*. Glasgow, 1961.

John Holt and Co.

John Holt and Co., a successful West African merchant house established in 1867, bought its first steamer (*Balmore*) in 1907 mainly to act as a tender for its river craft, although it did carry occasional cargo to and from West Africa. In 1909 the firm ordered two new ships, primarily to carry its own cargoes. It found it profitable and began a regular UK-West African service which only ended in the sale of its ships to Elder Dempster (Liner Holdings Ltd) in 1965. From 1950 it was re-named John Holt Line Ltd. and changed to the Guinea Gulf Line in 1954.

The museum holds the John Holt (Liverpool) Ltd. records which incorporated this merchant's shipping activities. It has only been roughly listed and will be covered in volume 2 of this guide. The collection includes models of *Balmore* (1890), *Jonathon Holt* (1910), and *John Holt* (1926).

Records

Minutes, photographs of launches, etc.
B/JH   c. 1876-1980   300 Boxes

Reference

Davies, P.N. *The Trade Makers. Elder Dempster in West Africa 1852-1972*. London, 1973.

Anon. "Guinea Gulf Line Ltd." *Sea Breezes*, New series, XXXI (1961), 264-275.

Inman Line

Founded in 1850 by Richardson Brothers and Co., with William Inman as partner, the Inman Line employed screw-propelled iron steamers from the outset and was the first steamship line to carry steerage passengers. Despite the loss of two ships and 480 passengers and crew in 1854 and the suspension of transatlantic sailings in favour of war work, 1854-1856, the line prospered, expanded and continued to innovate – for example, in the use of steam steering gear, lengthening existing ships (1869) and electric lighting (1879). From 1871 intense competition, especially from the White Star Line (started in 1871), the slump on the Atlantic from 1874 and increased shipbuilding costs caused problems. In 1881 its new liner, *City of Rome*, failed to meet specifications and was handed back to its builders; another vessel was wrecked in 1883 and in 1886 the Line was sold to the American International Navigation Co., owners of the American and Red Star Lines. This eventually led to American ownership in 1892 and the shift of the British terminus to Southampton in 1893.

The museum holds the model of *City of Paris* (1866). The Liverpool City Record Office also holds Inman records, including abstracts of logs of vessels, 1870-1875.

Records

Financial papers, newscuttings, etc. re: the formation of Inman Steamship Co. Ltd., including a prospectus re: purchase of bonds, and the liquidation of the company's assets, 1881-1886.
D/SO/7/1/40

Poster advertising the company's services to emigrants, 1874, in the Bryson Collection.
D/B/115GG

The Alsop Wilkinson Marine Solicitors collection contains financial Agreements, Deeds of Covenants etc. between the Inman Steam Ship Company Ltd. and Barrow Shipbuilding Co. re: repairs to *City of Rome*, 1884-1887, and agreements as to agency between the Inman Steam Ship Company and International Navigation Co. Ltd., 1885.
B/AW/29

Examples of the firm's stationery, tickets etc. can be found in the printer's example books of Turner and Dunnett.
SAS/31B/3/1-3/3

An Inman Line Steamship Company Official Guide for the Use of Passengers visiting Great Britain, Europe and the US and Canada. This includes illustrations of some of the vessels and a cabin plan of *City of Berlin*, c. 1878.
DX/934

Xerox copies of the memorandum of agreement for the foundation of the Inman
     Line, 1848-1849, the original proposal for its foundation, 1848, tables
     of statistics of earnings, 1863-1885, a painting of William Inman and
     a memento from *City of Richmond*.
DX/847

Discharge Certificates of Peter Davies who served on Inman Line vessels in the
     1870s.
SAS/23A/2/8

Reference

Bonsor, N.R.P. *North Atlantic Seaway. Vol. 2.* Jersey, 1978, 218-245.

The Irrawaddy Flotilla Co.

The Irrawaddy Flotilla and Burmese Steam Navigation Co. Ltd. was formed in
1865 to implement a contract with the government of India for the conveyance
of HM troops and mails on the Irrawaddy, together with general traffic from
Rangoon to Mandalay. The company made a notable contribution to the
development of Burma. In 1875 the services were incorporated as the Irrawaddy
Flotilla Company Ltd. with a fleet of thirteen steamers and twenty-nine flats.
Progress was rapid and by 1938 the fleet comprised some 600 vessels of all
descriptions from large paddle steamers to small buoying launches on 1300 miles
of difficult waterway. In a normal year prior to the Second World War the
company carried over eight million passengers and 1.25 million tons of cargo.
During the Japanese invasion of Burma in 1942 practically the whole fleet was
deliberately scuttled and the company was wound up in 1950 after its assets had
been transferred to the newly independent Burmese Government.

     The company was closely associated with British and Burmese Steam
Navigation Co. (see Henderson Line). The albums were compiled by Captain
H.J. Chubb of the Flotilla. The negatives are held by the National Maritime
Museum which also has a substantial number of plans of Flotilla vessels in its
Denny Collection.

Records

Three albums with over 700 photographs of ships, staff, office and other
     buildings, industrial and commercial scenes, cargoes being loaded and
     discharged, c. 1860-1945, design for handbook cover issued for British
     Empire Expedition, 1924, and share certificate, 1945.

D/IR   c. 1855-1945   3 Boxes

Photographs, booklets, charts, etc., 1865-1973.
DX/SAS

Three 5-inch tapes of Captain H.J. Chubb's reminiscences, recorded 1971.

Reference

Chubb, H.J. and Duckworth, C.L.D. *The Irrawaddy Flotilla Company*. London, 1973.

McCrae, A. and Prentice, A. *Irrawaddy Flotilla*. Paisley, 1978.

Johnston Warren Line

George Warren, Liverpool agent of the US White Diamond Line of sailing packets, took it over in 1857 and started a line of chartered steamers in 1865 to replace the obsolete sailing packets. This stopped between 1873 and 1875. It resumed with its own new ships in the latter year and prospered as an emigrant and cattle carrier. In 1898 it became a limited liability company (White Diamond Steamship Co. Ltd.) and was acquired by Furness Withy in 1912.

The Johnston Line, established in 1873, was a successful steamer service to the Levant and Black Sea. In 1880 it started an Atlantic service between Liverpool and Baltimore (later extended to Boston and Montreal). In 1916 it was purchased by Furness Withy and merged with the Warren Company in 1934. The Johnston Warren Line continued both routes and sustained heavy losses in the Second World War. The cargo-passenger service across the Atlantic finished in 1965 and the Mediterranean-Black Sea service went in 1970. The records are all located in the PSNC Archives. The museum holds models of Johnston's *Sagamore* (whale back steamer, 1893), *Pinemore* (1898), *Barnsmore* (1898) and Johnston Warren's *Nova Scotia* (1948).

Records

White Diamond Steamship Co. minutes, 1898-1935.
Articles of association, 1898, Extraordinary General Meetings, 1919.
George Warren and Co. (Liverpool) Ltd. minutes, 1912-1923.
Johnston Line, historical notes, minutes of board meetings, etc. 1912-1944.
Claims book, 1924-1961.
B/PSNC
Emigrant's Journal on *Fred Warren*, 1867.
DX/651
Printed ephemera from Black Sea and Atlantic trades, c. 1900-c. 1965.
D/WIT   2 Boxes

Reference

Middlemiss, N.L. *Furness-Houlder Lines*. Newcastle, 1991.

Lamport and Holt Line

Founded in 1845 by W.L. Lamport from Workington and George Holt (elder brother of Alfred of Blue Funnel fame), this partnership owned wooden sailing vessels trading with North and South America, South Africa and India. After some tentative involvement with steamers with James Moss and Co. and Papayanni Brothers in the Mediterranean in the mid-1850s, two 1300-ton tramp steamers were bought in 1861-1862. The Liverpool, Brazil and River Plate Steam Navigation Co. Ltd. was successfully started in 1865 to run cargo, mail and passenger services from Liverpool, London, Antwerp and Glasgow. In 1869 it pioneered the Brazil-New York coffee trade. In 1874 (the year of Lamport's death; Holt lived until 1896), no less than twelve new ships had been delivered or were building; the firm became a limited company and a Belgian subsidiary was created. Sailings were extended to Valparaiso in the 1880s (given up in 1896) and frozen meat transport from the River Plate was started in 1886. Live cattle were still carried and in 1898 five large (5555-ton) purpose-built ships were ordered. In 1902 a New York-South American passenger service was started with two second-hand ships and proved so successful that large new luxury liners were ordered. In 1910 three further (of over 10,000-tons) vessels built to a similar standard were ordered for the Liverpool route. This stimulated its biggest rival (Royal Mail) to take it over in 1911. At the outbreak of war in 1914 Lamport owned thirty-six ships of 200,000 tons, eleven of which were sunk. It reverted to cargo (especially frozen meat) as its staple trade except for the New York passenger business. But this was virtually wiped out by the bad publicity from the sinking of *Vestris* in 1928 and the 1929 Crash. Lamport collapsed along with the rest of Kylsant's Royal Mail group, was reconstituted in 1934, and sold to the Vestey Group (Blue Star Line) in 1944. It survived as a separate company until 1974. The last ship to operate under Lamport colours was the container ship *Churchill*.

  The sailmaker's plans are fragile, but there are microfilm copies available. The museum holds models of *Titian* (1902), *Verdi* (1907), *Vauban* (1912), and *Delius* (1937).

Records

Board minutes, etc., 1911-1955.
Liverpool, Brazil and River Plate Steam Navigation Co. Ltd.. minutes, 1908-1977.
Director's attendance register, 1934-1956.

Letterbooks, 1927-1940; Private letterbooks, 1912-1918.
Articles of association, 1865, 1911-1913.
Investment records, 1925-1945.
Tenancy agreements, etc., 1907-1942.
Financial records, ledgers, etc., 1895-1949.
Journals, 1905-1979.
Balance sheets/profit and loss accounts, 1910-1936.
Lord Kylsant crisis papers, 1930-1936.
Operational records, test certificates 1872-1949.
Copies of ships' registers, 1871-1962.
Buenos Aires and Montevideo shipping registers, 1889-1899.
Bills of sale, ship mortgages, etc., c. 1870-c. 1940.
Navigational and radio equipment agreements, 1927-1945.
Voyage results, 1911-1912.
New York commissions, 1908-1913.
Staff records, masters' and mates' certificates, 1871-1897.
Apprenticeship indentures, 1912-1918.
Miscellaneous papers, 1799-1951, including some photographs.

Records of Subsidiary or Connected Companies

Anglo-South American Airline Ltd.

Directors' attendance book, 1943-1957.
Certificate of incorporation, 1943.
Minutes of meetings, c. 1945-1950.
Correspondence, 1943-1957.

H. and W. Nelson (see Nelson Line)

B/LAH   1799, 1865-1979   48 Boxes

Sail plans of most nineteenth-century vessels, Eills and Co., sailmakers,
        Liverpool
SAS/   c. 1865-1890   2 Volumes

Reference

Heaton, P.M. *Lamport and Holt*. Newport, 1986.

Board of Trade. *Vestris Inquiry*. London, 1929.

Lancashire Shipping Co.

James Chambers (died 1877), a former partner of White Star (Australian) Line, established Lancaster Shipowners' Co., which was wound up in 1896. Its assets were incorporated by his son, W.J. Chambers, into the Lancashire Shipping Co., which tramped and ran the Castle Line from Europe to the Gulf of Mexico and on a round-the-world service with the American Barber Line. After the First World War activity shifted to services between Liverpool, New York, Cuba and Mexico plus tramp voyages to Asia and the Pacific. It lost five of its nine ships in the Second World War and in 1944 was sold to Mollers Trust Ltd. of Hong Kong. W.J. Chambers (died 1923), was a member of the MDHB from 1903 to 1923 and was chairman of the Pilotage Committee, 1913-1923.

Records

Memorandum and articles of association registered, 1896.
Directors' and managers' report, 1919 and 1934.
Articles of partnerships, 1921 and 1928.
Share agreements, 1923.
Schedules of vessels, 1897-1918.
SAS/29/12/1-9   1 Box

Reference

McRoberts, J. "Chambers' Castle Line." *Sea Breezes*, New series, XLVII, 359, 427, 490, 577.

Thomas, P.N. *British Ocean Tramps. Vol. 2.* Wolverhampton, 1992, 84-86.

Larrinaga and Co.

This business was established at Liverpool in 1862 by three Basques to run sailing ships under the Spanish flag. In 1870 a regular line of cargo and passenger steamers was started between Liverpool and the Philippines, followed by a line between Liverpool and Cuba. In 1896 a regular service was established between Galveston and Manchester. The company began to register its ships in Liverpool after the Spanish-American War. Much of its business in the twentieth century was tramping in the grain trade and by the 1960s it was the last ocean tramp shipping company in Liverpool.

The museum holds three ship portraits and some of the furnishings of the family home in Liverpool are in the China Trade collection of Liverpool Museum.

Records

Thirteen undated documents, all in Spanish, c. 1780-1850.
Thirty-two dated documents, all in Spanish, 1784-1873 (the latest written from
        Liverpool).
Plans of ships, 1863-1901.
Copies of registration documents and Lloyd's certificates, 1859-1901.
Photographs, c. 1865-c. 1960.
B/LAR   1784-1901   2 Boxes

Reference

Thomas, P.N. *British Ocean Tramps. Vol. 2.* Wolverhampton, 1922, 90.

Leyland Line

Frederick Leyland joined Bibby Son and Co. in the 1840s, rising to become a
junior partner in 1859 when Bibby was in the Mediterranean trade. Frederick
Leyland pressed the company to provide a Liverpool and Boston service. The
family directors opposed him with the result that Frederick Leyland in 1873
bought the company, putting ships on the North Atlantic yet retaining the
Mediterranean interest. On Frederick Leyland's sudden death in 1892 the firm
was taken over by Christopher Furness and made a limited liability company.
In 1896 the Leyland Line joined a new North Atlantic consortium comprised of
the Wilson Line of Hull and Furness Withy and Co. to run a London, Boston
and New York passenger and cargo service independently of their existing
services. In 1899 it bought the Liverpool-based West Indian and Pacific Line.
In 1901 the new American combine, IMM, bought the Leyland Lines' Atlantic
services; and Ellerman the Mediterranean fleet. Under IMM ownership Leyland
was run down in favour of White Star and by the end of the First World War
was largely a cargo service. In 1933 it was sold to Vestey Brothers and its fleets
disposed of to various owners. The *Californian* of *Titanic* fame was one of its
ships and its master's papers (Captain Lord) are listed in Special Collections (see
volume 2). The museum has a model of *Hanoverian* (1903).

Records

Twenty-one single steamship company contracts for sale of Leyland Line ships
        to the executors of F.R. Leyland, November 1892.
D/B115/11   1 Box

Volumes (2) of Captain's Report on Officers, c. 1875-1930.
DX/865   1 Box

Reference

Bonsor, N.R.P. *North Atlantic Seaway. Vol. 2.* Jersey, 1978, 797-798, 847-848.

J.J. Mack and Sons Ltd.

J.J. Mack, coastal shipowner, shipping and forwarding agent, was founded in Liverpool in the 1880s. In 1891 it started the Belfast and Mersey Steamship Co. in competition with the established Belfast Steamship Co., and with the opening of the Manchester Ship Canal extended its service as the Belfast, Mersey and Manchester Steamship Company. It was taken over by Coast Lines in 1945 but continued separate sailings until 1959, after which it acted as agent for the Belfast S.S. Co. until 1969. The Mack family also had interests in Alexandra Towing Co. and United Grain Elevator Co. A model of *Fleswick* (1900) is also in the museum's collection.

Records

Minute books, 1928-1939.
Balance sheets, 1929-1942.
Records of Belfast, Mersey & Manchester S.S. Co. Ltd. include papers re: appointment of managers, 1891, 1929-1934.
Articles of association, 1891 and 1929.
Minutes of meetings, 1932.
Balance sheets, 1929-1943.
Wages and insurance books, 1934-1940.
DX/220   c. 1891-1940   4 Boxes

Reference

Sinclair, R.C. *Across the Irish Sea, Belfast-Liverpool Shipping since 1819.* London, 1990.

John S. Monks Ltd.

J. and J. Monk and Co. set up as a coastal owner at Preston in 1907, moving to Liverpool in 1909. On the death of James Monks, it was re-registered as John S. Monks in 1924. Its staple cargoes were coal, grain and steel. Coastal traffic declined in the early 1960s and the firm went into liquidation after the loss of the Workington steel contract in 1963. There are five models of Monks' steam coasters in the museum's collection as well as a painting and photographs.

Records

Directors' minute book, 1907-1912.
Cargo books (3), 1921-1955.
Pamphlet, *50 years of J.S. Monks', 1907-1957*
SAS/29/16/5-9   1 Box

Reference

Fenton, R. *Monks's Navy*. Kendal, 1984.

National Line

Founded in Liverpool in 1863, National Steam Navigation Co. Ltd. concentrated on a fleet of large iron screw steamers for the cargo and emigrant trade from Liverpool to New York. In 1867 it was reorganised to meet the challenge of the new Guion Line set up by its former passenger agent. The policy of capacity rather than speed was pursued. Three vessels, lengthened and fitted with compound engines, 1870-1872, and new vessels were among the biggest in the world – for example, the 4169-ton *Italy* of 1870. That was also the year the Line carried 33,500 steerage passengers and 395,000 tons of cargo, which put it ahead of Cunard, Guion and Anchor and just behind Inman. The Line stagnated in the late-1870s; several attempts to establish new services failed and in 1879 four of its twelve ships were taken as military transport for the Zulu War. In 1884 the Line made its only attempt on the Blue Riband with the elegant new *America* (5528 tons). It succeeded, but only for two months. The ship was expensive to run and was sold at a loss in 1887. The museum has a splendid model of it. Although the years 1887-1889 were reasonably profitable, there was a drop in traffic in 1890 and a loss of two ships in six months. The Liverpool passenger service was ended and replaced with a cargo-only London-New York service. The Line was bought by the Atlantic Transport Line in 1896 and operated separately until its disappearance in 1914.

Records

Sailing bills for the National Line's Liverpool-New York service, with
    illustrations of SS *England* and SS *Helvetia*, c. 1870.
SAS/33F/3/9

Advertisements for sailing, c. 1875-1880.
SAS/33F/3/1

Some papers in the Bryson collection including a Director's report and statement
     of accounts, 1872; resolution of the Board re: an agreement made
     between Atlantic trade competitors, 1875; and share transfer certificates
     and dividends, 1873-1875.
D/B/115

Reference

Bonsor, N.R.P. *North Atlantic Seaway. Vol. 2.* Jersey, 1978, 599-615.

Nelson Line

Hugh Nelson, son of an Irish butcher who moved to Liverpool to import Irish
cattle, went to the Argentine to establish a meat plant to supply his father's
shops. To transport the frozen meat a shipping line was established in 1897,
which resulted in a regular River Plate-Liverpool service that from 1898 was
known as the Nelson Line (Liverpool) Ltd. Between 1901 and 1904 seven new
large ships with passenger accommodation were added and were followed by
another ten in 1910 for the Nelson Line (London) Ltd. In 1913 Sir Owen
Philipps' Royal Mail group bought up all the Nelson ships but kept it as a
separate business. In 1928-1929 the Line took delivery of five innovative
14,000-ton motorships, which were absorbed into the restructured Royal Mail
Lines Ltd. in 1932 after the collapse of Royal Mail. They retained their original
Nelson Highland names. The Archives are part of the Lamport and Holt
collection. The museum has a large half-model of *Highland Monarch* (1928).

Records

Letters, 1924-1930.
B/LAH   1 Box

Reference

Bonsor, N.R.P. *South Atlantic Seaway.* Jersey, 1983, 361-368.

Philip Nelson

Philip Nelson was a Liverpool-based master mariner, shipbroker and owner
from Maryport with whom T.H. Ismay (see Oceanic Steam Navigation Co.
entry) was in partnership between 1856 and 1863. In 1863 Ismay set up his own
business and eventually re-launched the White Star Line as a transatlantic
steamship service in 1871. These are part of the records of a descendant, the
late Dr. Philip Nelson, a collector of antiquities well known in Liverpool.

The museum has a model of *Ann Nelson* (1849).

Records

Letterbooks (indexed), containing many references to specific vessels, including list of stores for *Humphrey Nelson*, ships' costs, voyages to Brazil, Argentina, Chile, Honolulu, Shanghai, San Francisco, references to launch of *Philip Nelson* (1864) and disposal of *Admiral Nelson* (1865).

B/N   1856-1872   1 Box

Reference

Anderson, R. *White Star*. Prescot, 1964, 40-41.

Ocean Steam Ship Co. and its Successor

The Ocean Steam Ship Co. (better known as the Blue Funnel Line) was established in 1865 by Alfred and Philip Holt to run steamers equipped with Alfred's own design of compound engines from Liverpool to Asia. Steamers had not been sufficiently economical hitherto to compete with the tea clippers in this lucrative but distant trade. After some initial difficulties, the company's fortunes were boosted by the opening of the Suez Canal in 1869 which reduced the distance and was not accessible to sailing ships. In the next decade the Holts expanded their services with the assistance of Butterfield and Swire, their agents in Shanghai, and were prime movers in establishing the first Far Eastern Conference in 1879. Holts continued to expand their feeder services, for example, to Sumatra for the tobacco trade. Between 1882 and 1893 it was in severe competition with the China Mutual Steam Navigation Co. (see separate entry). In 1891 it established a Dutch subsidiary to run a direct service from Amsterdam to Indonesia. Three years later it extended its Singapore feeder services as far as Fremantle. This was followed by a direct UK-Australia service in 1901. By 1911 (the year of Alfred Holt's death) the company had acquired China Mutual and owned sixty-two ships. Acquisitions continued including Royden's India Line 1915 and Greenshield Cowie's Knight Line in 1917. Wartime action caused the loss of twelve ships. The 1920s proved difficult – for example, reduced demand in the Australian passenger business led to a joint service with White Star in 1924. In 1932 Holts obtained effective control of Elder Dempster Lines and in 1935 the Glen and Shire Lines and the Straits S.S. Co. (in which it had a substantial stake already) were acquired. Forty-one ships were lost in the Second World War (no less than eighteen in 1941). Peacetime services were resumed with stop-gap Liberty ships for many sailings until twenty-one A-class replacements were delivered between 1946 and 1953. Holts maintained their formidable position in Asia until the 1970s. Their future to an extent was secured by participation in the Overseas Container Lines consortium, set up in 1965 and from 1972 (marked by a change of name to Ocean Transport and Trading Co.), it diversified away from deep-sea shipping with the takeover of the Cory fuel distribution group. New shipping activities included Ocean Inchcape Ltd., operating offshore supply vessels (1971), the purchase of bulkers, tankers and gas carriers and the Barber Blue Sea transpacific ro-ro service. But by 1987 these and the traditional Holt cargo liners, as well as the holdings in OCL (except for Ocean Inchcape Ltd.), had been disposed of.

The collection provides a good record of the development of the parent company. Voyage books, freight accounts, statements of depreciation, earnings, taxation and staff records extend in depth over a hundred years. This entry also includes the records of the Dutch subsidiary and the recent activities of Ocean Transport and Trading. There is an unlisted collection of Barber Blue Sea Line records as well as other Ocean material mainly on finance and sea staff received in 1993. General arrangements of many Blue Funnel Ships can be found in the SAS collection of plans.

Other companies are separately treated under the following heads: African Steamship Co.; British & African S.N. Co.; China Mutual Steam Navigation Co.; William Cory & Son Ltd.; Elder Dempster Lines; Glen and Shire Lines; Henderson Line; Hull Blyth (see volume 2); and Straits Steamship Co. Ltd.

This collection was originally catalogued and indexed by the company's honourary archivist. The primary record is a card index with numbers that bear no relation to the archival structure; for example, the annual meetings minute books, report and accounts are all numbered 4003. What is available for consultation is in fact a "classified index" under seventeen heads. It includes many printed publications which are not Archives. There is overlap between the various categories and it is hard to see why many of the records are classified as they are. Unfortunately, it is unlikely to be re-catalogued or re-indexed in the near future. Researchers should, therefore, scan the catalogue and card indices widely and not be surprised to find many references to the affairs of one company in the Archives of another, particularly in that of the main company, Ocean. Fortunately, there are published histories of a number of the companies which will help. The entries for the various companies in the Ocean Group will sometimes do less than justice to the depth and variety of the records.

Records

Secretarial (Ocean S.S. Co)

Minute books, annual meetings, with reports and accounts, 1866-1955.
Managers' minute books, 1902-1980.
Directors' meetings minutes, 1957 onwards.

Finance Committee, 1973-1976.
Articles of association, 1865.
Annual reports and accounts, 1965-1966.
Filmed annual reports, 1976-1980.
Investment papers, 1910-1976.
Register of members, 1903-1956.
Material on legislation, including A. Holt's evidence to Board of Trade, 1874.
Requisition of vessels, World War I.
Legal opinions, judgements, etc., 1942-1958.
Merger letters, A. Holt and Co./Glen Line, 1935.

Financial

Ledgers, 1853-1914.
Prime costs of vessels, 1921-1963.
Final costs, 1913-1917, 1944-1952.
Birkenhead accounts book, 1913-1957.
Freight ledger, 1938-1943.
Ships, ledgers, voyage books, 1897-1902.
Managers' commissions, depreciation statements, 1908-1947.
Captains, commissions, ditto, 1934-1947.

Management

Files relating to leading management personalities, including Holts, Bruce
    Glasier, Sir Sydney Jones, Sir John Hobhouse, Sir John Nicholson, Sir
    Lindsay Alexander, R.H. Thornton, etc., c. 1870-1980.

Reports, notes, etc., by senior managers on various subjects, e.g., UK South
    coast ports, Australian and Asian ports, dock labour, Dutch ports,
    stevedorage, air cargo economics, various management issues including
    ship management, security, fleet operation, Rochdale Report, Suez
    Canal, China visitors and cruise ships, c. 1915-1985.

Correspondence

Mainly re: overseas property and affairs, also includes early letters, references
    to Singapore, Melbourne, Kowloon, Indonesia, Shanghai, Yokohama
    (earthquake), South Africa, Chinese crews, Suez Canal, trading with
    the enemy (World War II), c. 1870-1980.

Speeches and Addresses

Mainly 1950-1956.

Staff

Directions to Captain Middleton, master on *Agamemnon*'s first voyage, 1866; shore staff (including overseas), mostly 1955-1980.
Papers on office organisation including staff handbook.
References to principals of Aulis training establishment; appointments of senior staff, shore staff files, 1872-1977.
Nestorian Association minute books, 1962-1975.
Salary and establishment surveys, 1969, 1972, etc.
Deck officers registers, c. 1890-c. 1920.
Officers' reminiscences, etc. c. 1880-1960.
Engineers' records, 1888-1949.
Stewards records, 1914-1957.
Carpenters' records, c. 1920 onwards.
Chinese crews, miscellaneous papers, c. 1945-c. 1970.
Seamen's strike, 1960-1961.
Medical staff records, 1940-c. 1960.
Wages Books, 1868-1967 (one of the finest surviving series).
Papers re: training, c. 1960-c. 1970.
Superannuation and pension records, 1910-1977.

Cargo

Pooling rules, 1913.
Agreements, Australian, Conference and trade, c. 1890-c. 1960.
Minutes, Far Eastern and Indonesian Trade Division, 1973-1975.
Marine Committee minutes, 1974-1979.
Far East Conference minutes, 1918-1940.
Papers re: services to Japan, 1872.
Stevedoring agreements, 1912-1951.
Charter parties, 1958-1961.
America, China, Australia, Far East, various papers re: cargo services.
Stowage plans, 1924-1975.
Port logbooks, 1960-1975.
Bills of lading (selected) c. 1940-c. 1970.
Sample manifestos, 1972-1976.
Movements of freight, 1901-1919.
Blue Funnel tonnages, 1923-1964.
Voyage results, 1935-1949.

Steamer earnings, 1876-1967.

Carryings and earnings, 1930-1968.

Outward cargo tonnages and net freight, summary c. 1950-c. 1968; freight statistics, c. 1950-c. 1960.

Freight tariffs for areas in the Middle and Far East, incomplete voyage, 1937-1972.

Passengers

Far Eastern Passenger Conference Agreements, 1954.

Advertising, 1938.

Depassengerisation; enquiry into future of certain classes of ships, 1962-1963.

Passenger Literature, 1892.

Cruise brochures and passenger lists, 1923-1924.

Passengers aboard *Phemius* when lost, 1943.

Chinese passengers, piracy, 1928.

Papers re: pilgrims to Mecca (including photographs), 1929-1961.

Trade, General

Files on air cargoes, 1966-c. 1975; Suez Canal, 1936-1964; tallow, uranium, latex, tobacco, Tasmanian apples, copra, frozen cargoes, carbon black, timber, rubber, c. 1950-1980; containerisation, 1951-1967; German agencies, 1921.

Fleet

Ships journals, 1866-1974 (virtually complete).

Other records are extremely extensive (mostly 1910 onwards) particularly full for the Second World War and postwar.

Wireless code books, pre-1938.

Shipbuilding records, c. 1885-1978, including drawings, specifications, agreements, papers on specific issues, engine arrangements, 1885-1895.

Papers re: *Phemius* typhoon salvage 1932; fires on various ships, 1953-1969.

Suez Canal problems, 1964-1968.

Incidents in China, 1949, 1968, 1970.

Publicity

Press reports, 1944-1977.

Publicity material and ephemera, c. 1920-c. 1970 including calendars, diaries, and menus.

Sailing cards and notices, 1866-c. 1970.

Promotional films, 1965-1968.

Property

Papers relating to company property, Birkenhead, Liverpool and overseas, 1912-1980.

House Magazines

Halfdeck (midshipman's magazine), 1956-1966.
Staff Bulletin, 1940-1967.
Ocean, 1967-1979.
Ocean Mail, 1970-c. 1985.
Nestorian, 1984 to date (Library).

Photographs

Ships, directors, captains, port scenes, c. 1860-c. 1980.
Tape recordings of long serving staff members, c. 1970.

Other Unofficial Records

There is a large amount of this material, including personal reminiscences, the diary of Captain Kidd, first master of *Ajax* (1845); diary of Philip Wearing, steward on *Nestor*, 1875; reminiscences of G.A. Pridgeon, a dock worker, 1887-1940.

It also includes virtually all books, articles and papers, published and unpublished, which were relevant to company history.

OA　　　1845-c. 1990　　　　　1040 Boxes　　　288 Volumes

Reference

Falkus, M. *The Blue Funnel Legend. A History of Ocean Steam Ship Company, 1865-1973*. London, 1990.

Haws, D. *Blue Funnel Line*. Hereford, 1984.

Pacific Steam Navigation Co.

Pacific Steam Navigation Co. (PSNC) was set up by royal charter in 1840 to run steamer services on the west coast of South America. William Wheelwright, an American master mariner and shipbroker with experience of operating steamers in South America, inspired its foundation, was appointed Chief Superintendent in 1840, and took overall control after a dispute with the original directors in 1843. PSNC successfully overcame all the problems of operating on a distant 4000-mile coastline with many navigational hazards and few facilities. It was quick to take up technical innovations such as iron hulls (1845) and compound engines (1856). After a dispute with the Panama Railway Co., it started a direct Liverpool-Valparaiso service from 1868. By 1873 it had the biggest merchant steamer fleet in the world (fifty-seven vessels) but an over-ambitious weekly Liverpool-Callao timetable caused losses and cut-backs in 1874-1875. In 1877 six of its laid-up steamers were used on a new London-Australia service in partnership with Anderson, Anderson and Co.; this became the Orient Line which was eventually sold to the Royal Mail group in 1906. The South American services continued to be its main focus and these were beset by local wars, leading to economic disruption, competition and the navigational hazards which led to a continual loss of ships. Nevertheless, it was able to maintain its strong position, helped by an extension of its charter and the modernisation of its fleet, which began to include larger luxury passenger liners such as the *Orcoma* ("the electric ship") of 1908. In 1910 the rapidly expanding Royal Mail bought PSNC, but it continued to operate separately with its existing policies.

In the First World War its ships served as transports, hospital ships and armed merchant cruisers; eleven were lost. The opening of the Panama Canal in 1914 intensified competition, especially with US lines to Ecuador, Peru and Chile. PSNC countered after the war by starting a New York-South America service and building five new motor cargo ships. In 1922 Chile decided to reserve its coastal trade, which was a major blow. The Royal Mail group collapsed in 1931 and PSNC was rescued. Apart from its 20,000-ton express passenger liner, *Reina del Pacifico*, its ships were slow, aging and reduced to a total of fourteen by 1938. Renewals, ordered in 1939, were held up by the outbreak of the Second World War. Five new ships were delivered between 1943 and 1948.

The new tonnage and an extended route with an increased number of calls at Caribbean ports saw a revival in the 1950s and early 1960s but jet aircraft reduced passenger traffic, while competition from subsidised national shipping lines affected cargo. In 1960-1961 two tankers were purchased. In 1965 PSNC and Royal Mail were bought by Furness Withy. Conventional cargo services were gradually phased out in favour of combi-vessels and in 1983 a single container ship as part of a consortium. In 1980 Furness Withy, including PSNC, was taken over by Hong Kong shipowner C.Y. Tung and re-sold to the German Oetker shipping group.

Some files may relate to a number of associated companies and it has not always been possible to distinguish each one precisely. The companies involved are Royal Mail Steam Packet Company (RMSP), Furness Withy, Johnston Line, White Diamond Line, George Warren and Co. (Liverpool) Ltd.

and Shaw Savill. Material which can be clearly identified as relating to the above companies will be found under that company's appropriate heading but cross-referenced to the PSNC Archives, where it will continue to be kept.

Records

Chartered and Parliamentary

Charters and Supplements 1840, 1846, 1859, 1865, 1867, 1873, 1875, 1881, 1902, 1922, 1983.
Printed copies of charters, 1840-1922.
Memorial to the Treasury re: shares issue, 1863, 1871.
Act for reduction of capital, 1878 and supporting papers.

Administration

Board minutes, 1838-1953; Draft minutes, 1872-1874.
General Meeting minutes, 1843-1969.
General Meeting of shareholders, transcript, 1874; reports of Annual Meetings, 1874-1953.
Management Committee minutes, 1963-1965.
Semi-private letterbooks, 1873-1936.
Directors attendance books, 1929-1950.
Reports of directors, 1861-1964.
Prospectus (in Spanish) 1836.
Prospectus (in English) 1838.
Letter and report of William Wheelwright to Directors of PSNC, 1846-1847.
Documents relating to the foundation of PSNC, 1838-1843.

Conference and Joint Committees

Minutes of West Indian/Atlantic Steamship companies, 1914-1916.
Magellan and West Coast of South America Associated Lines Committee, 1921-1923.
Callao Sub-committee of European/South Pacific and Magellan Conference, 1926-1933.
European/South Pacific and Magellan Conference Organisation, 1939-1940, 1944-1947 and 1949-1950.
PSNC/RMS Joint Committee minutes, 1916-1923.
British Government Liner Tonnage Conference, 1947-1948.

Legal and Property

Mersey Docks and Harbour Board v. PSNC re: SS *Orita*, 1924.
Rules & By-laws, 1864-1910.
Leases (including RMSP) of property in Panama, 1924-1959.
Conveyances of property in Panama, 1851-1923, and in Tobago and Morro
    Islands, 1851-1942.
Licence agreements, 1915-1954.
Estate papers (various ports of mid and south America, 1918-1950).
Official seal register, 1898-1963.
Register of documents in secretary's safe, 1925.
Contracts and agreements, 1916-1942.
Deed, Nile S.S. Co. and PSNC, 1965-1966.
Plan of headquarters, James St. (Pacific Building), Liverpool, 1948, 1966.
Papers re: Mortgage of MV *Reina del Pacifico*, 1931-1934; *Loretta* collision
    case, 1942.

Investment

Share register, 1912-1916.
Share certificate book, 1840-1853.
Register of proxies, 1845-1896.
Register of debentures, 1931-1941.
Trust deed for securing debenture stock, 1931.

Financial

Annual accounts, 1875-1900.
Companies Act annual returns, 1928-1949.
Balance sheets, 1873-1964.
Reports of directors and statement of accounts, 1873-1965.
Depreciation figures, 1929-1951.
Credit/debit ledger, 1929-1976.
Audit files, 1964-1970.
Profit and loss accounts, 1950-1964.
Ledgers, personal, 1923-1936; impersonal, 1923-1929; west coast, 1923-1929;
    voyage, 1928-1929; private insurance, 1928-1932; private, 1933-1974.
Liverpool cash receipts and disbursements, 1928-1940.
Report on reconstruction proposals by Thomson McLintock and Co., 1934.

Management

Report on postwar economic crisis, 1921-1929.

General letters file, 1969-1978.
Running costs breakdown, 1932.
Shipping statistics, 1936-1979.
Report on visit to New York, Havana, Kingston (Jamaica), Cristobal and West
        Coast of South America, 1939.
"Missed Opportunities!" Critique of PSNC Management, 1942.
General Manager's Committee precis, 1923-1936.
File re: W.C. Warwick's visit to Lima, Peru, 1954.
Files re: W.H. Davies' visit to South America, 1946.
Correspondence re: political and legal situation in Peru, 1942.
Report re: effects on competition, 1939.
File re: Imperial Shipping Committee and passenger taxes, 1947-1949.
File re: possible sale of *Orbita* and *Orduna* to a Greek company, 1949.
Chairman's file re: hold ventilation, 1949-1950.
File re: naming of ships, 1951.
Correspondence re: project at Mejillones, Chile, 1912-1937, and re: Cuidad
        Trujillo (Dominican Republic) as trading post, 1945.
Correspondence re: purchase of Silver Line ships, 1949-1951.
File re: trade depression, 1921.
Files re: financial crisis (Lord Kylsant) 1931-1938.
File containing correspondence with P.G.M. Mitchell, RMSP, re: war bonus
        and relations with Peru, 1933-1942.
File re: T.H. Darlington, Panama Canal agent, 1942-1948.
Correspondence, W.H. Davies and Sir Ernest Murrant, 1949-1950.
Minutes of General Manager's meeting, 1919-1920.
Files including Antofagasta Railway Co.; Arbuckle, Smith and Co. Ltd.;
        Anglo-Iranian Oil Co.; British Paints; Johnston Line; Houlder Bros.;
        McGregor, Gow and Holland; Arnot and Sons Ltd.; Falkland Islands
        Co. Ltd.; Hamburg-Amerika Line; Blythe Dry Docks and Shipbuilding
        Co. Ltd.; Flota Mercante Gran Colombiane; Balfour Williamson and
        Co.; Port of Liverpool Stevedoring Co.; Glen Line; John I. Jacob and
        Co., 1934-1952.

Insurance (See also Financial)
Analysis of underwriting account, 1925-1932.
Policy for voyage on *Orbita*, Liverpool to Buenos Aires, 1920.
File re: fleet insurance, 1938-1944.

Operational

Tonnage and freight, 1961-1970.
Standing dock instructions, 1924-1959.
SS *Cotapaxi*, instruction to commanders, 1950.

Commanders, voyage instructions, 1874-1971.
Instructions to office staff, 1917-1948.
Papers re: agencies (RMSP and PSNC), 1918-1956.
Sailing list, 1874-1981.
Charter party agreements, 1854, 1963-1964, 1969, 1973.
Bill of lading, 1838.
Head office departmental arrangements, 1872.
Agency volumes, 1951-1978.
Indemnities book, 1944-1959.
Index to port agents and ports, P-Z, 1911-1955.
Bareboat charter, *Samothrace*, 1947.
Voyage accounts for each vessel, 1946-1973.
Correspondence, including complaints, 1928-1950.
Correspondence re: oil discharge, 1934-1935.
File re: passenger travelling requirements, 1949-1951.
File re: freight contracts, 1951.
File re: accounts of various ships, 1944.
File re: crossing to Bermuda and competition from Caronia, 1948-1949.
Reports on agencies, c. 1895-1922.
North Pacific freight engagement book, 1937-1957.
File re: Cuba shipments, 1935-1945.
Tariff rates, 1930-1968.
Record of voyages, 1955-1962.
File re: meat berth, Huskisson Dock, 1943-1947.

Staff

Salaries and wages, 1902-c. 1912.
Crew books, 1916-1973.
Record of employees, 1899-1954.
Record of employees, purser's department, 1921-1969.
Crew sick book, 1952.
Engineer officers records, 1963-1971 (including RMSP and Furness Withy).
Benevolent fund accounts, 1911-1940.
Register of accidents, 1919-1923.
Engineer's contracts of service, 1846-1866.
Diary (copy) of voyage of Dr. J.M. Ryan, ship's surgeon, 1877-1878.
Miscellaneous career papers, 1888-1923.
Dock staff file, 1920-1962.
Register of salary payments, 1954-1956.
PSNC superannuation, reports of committee of management and financial statements, 1963-1977.
Actuarial papers, 1961-1971.

Pamphlet re: engineer cadet ship, c. 1960.
Rates of pay, 1917.
Correspondence re: personnel matters west coast staff, 1927-1928.
Records of officers, 1862-1912.
Records of engine department, 1916-1922.
Records of pursers' department, 1900-1928.
Records of deck department, 1879-1930.
Records of cadets, 1922-1952.
West coast records, deck department, 1887-1920.
Changes in crew's desertions, etc., 1917-1923.
Seniority books, officers, 1905-1917.
West coast pursers and assistants (with notes of nationality), c. 1895-1922.
Records of engineers' department, commercial marine, 1920-1930.
Records of cadets, commercial marine, 1923-1929.

Ships

Capacity plans, c.1953-c.1970.
Loading arrangements, 1972-1973.
Ships registers (copies) 1869-1945.
Sea trials MV *Oroya* and *Oropesa*, 1978.
Specifications, 1878 and 1919.
Collision, SS *Loreto*, 1941.
Contract for tanker, 1958.
Correspondence re: tanker *William Wheelwright*, 1958.
Specification, MV *Oroya*, *Oropesa*, 1978; *Reina de Mar*.
Special Issue, *Journal of Commerce*, 1956.
File re: chartering, etc., 1963-1969.
Berthing book, (9), 1962-1964.
General arrangement plan, c. 1962.
Sea Egg, correspondence, 1966.
Cotopaxi guard book, 1913-1966.
List of ships, 1860-1880.
Album, newscuttings and photograph, W.C. Warwick's tour from Liverpool to
        Plymouth via Cuba, Jamaica, Panama, Columbia, Ecuador, Peru, Chile
        on MV *Santander*, 1948, with supporting papers, 1948.
Correspondence re: *Reina del Mar*, 1954-1956.
File re: *Lobos* collision with Thomas B. Reed, 1945.
File re: *Reina del Pacifico* explosion, 1947.
File re: launch of SS *Kenuta*, 1950.
File re: grounding of MV *Sarmiento* off Cuba, 1951.
File on *Reina del Mar*'s shakedown cruise, 1955-1956.
File re: *Reina del Pacifico* voyage, 1947-1949.

File re: *Orduna* incidents, 1935.
File re: turbine of *Orbita*, 1948 and 1949.

Photographs

Launch albums (3) MV *Orbita, Orduna, Ortega*, 1972-1973.
Miscellaneous, including cruises, officers, operations, special occasions, mid
　　and South America, 1901-c. 1980 (including Furness Withy and
　　RMSP).
Portraits of founders, management, captains, officers etc., c. 1840-c. 1980.
Queen's Award to Industry, 1978.
Ships, c. 1882-1921, c. 1950-1980.
Sports events, 1922-1980.

House Magazines

Pacific Breezes, 1956-1957.
Pacific and Atlantic Breezes, 1972.
Sea Breezes, 1919-1937.

Historical Notes

Material relating to the foundation of the company, including newscuttings,
　　photographs, copies of documents, etc., 1938-1980.
Material, including designs, relating to the coats of arms of Royal Mail Steam
　　Packet Co. and PSNC.
Material re: Captain George Peacock, first captain of a PSNC vessel, 1980.
Articles and cuttings, 1921-1980.

Ephemera

Launch brochures, guest lists, accommodation plans, voyage itineraries, memos,
　　passenger lists, sailing cards, maps, tickets, timetables, brochures,
　　1877-1972. (N.B. a few items from other companies are included, e.g.,
　　RMSP and Elder Dempster).
Crossing the Equator and Arctic Circle.
Licences, diploma and proclamation, c. 1960-c. 1970; handbooks and tables, c.
　　1860-1885.
Christmas cards, 1946-1968.
Pocket diary, 1975.
Race card, MV *Santander* (Grand National).

World War I

Falkland Islands battle, 1914, other, 1966-1976.
Protocol from the Commander of a German commerce raider to the Captain of
    SS *Esmeraldas*, 1917.
Papers re: German raider *Moewe*, 1915 and 1918.
Journal of Commander W.H. Kelly, 1916-1918.
Documents regarding effects on trade with South America, 1915-1922.

World War II

Various papers including South America trade, 1935-1944.
Spanish booklet re: PSNC in World War II, 1946.
Correspondence from German activities in South America, 1941-1942.
File re: Chairman's visit to West Coast, including correspondence with Ministry
    of War Transport, 1944-1945.
File re: wartime arrangements, awards for bravery and US black list,
    1941-1947.

Miscellaneous

Certificate presented to master and crew of *Reina del Mar* in recognition of
    seventy-two transits of the Panama Canal, 1964.
125th anniversary of Punta Arenas, 1965.
Life of William Wheelwright (in Spanish) 1876.
List of PSNC and Chilean ships in Pacific, 1893.
Share certificate, Callao Dock Co., 1895.
Chilean National Anthem, 1906.
File re: coal strike in Liverpool, 1911-1912.
Memo Book of F. Alcock re: PSNC and RMSP in West Indies and Pacific
    1912-1914.
Draft document re: export of munitions to Bolivia via Africa, 1933.
Agency for BOAC, 1963-1965.
Maps of N., Mid. and S. America; U.K., Europe, (with charts, 1868-c.1930).
Newsletters, reports, advertisements, 1965-1980.
Miscellaneous newspapers, 1840-1955.
Proofs of *Steam Conquers the Pacific* by A.C. Wardle.
Automated Mutual Assistance Vessel Reserve Award Scheme, 1976-1978.
Ships' stamps, magazines, correspondence, etc., 1978-1980.
Papers re: twenty-five club (for employees with twenty-five years continuous
    service, 1970-1980).
Captain Dawson, Kingston, Jamaica, letter, 1813.
Documents relating to Panama (in Spanish), 1915.

Marine Display in the Mersey on occasion of Royal visit (brochure), 1913.
Newspapers on maritime PSNC themes, including Chilean, 1840, 1927-1955.
Historic facsimiles (1836 and 1854); PSNC Arts, Crafts and Hobbies Exhibition
   files, 1964.
North Sea Oil, Brent field, brochures, 1979-1980-1982.
Correspondence re: Lady Essendon's travelling arrangements, 1948-1949.
West Coast Leader, Peru English language newspaper, 1933-1934.
File re: new Havana agent's office, 1954.
Letter from General Sir S.F. Muspratt, 1956-1958.
Plan of Huskisson Dock, Liverpool.
B/PSNC   c. 1838-c. 1982   78 volumes   73 Boxes

References

Haws, D. *Pacific Steam Navigation Co.* Hereford, 1986.

Wardle, A.C. *Steam Conquers the Pacific. A Record of Maritime Achievement,
   1840-1940.* London, 1940.

Papayanni Line

George Papayanni, Greek emigré merchant, moved from London to Liverpool
in 1844, as he considered it a better centre for the Mediterranean trade. He took
as a partner a Turk, Pierre Massabini. The firm traded to the Levant (northeast
Mediterranean; Greece and Turkey), later extending to the whole of the eastern
Mediterranean. Papayanni and Massabini chartered steamers from 1846 and
owned them from 1855 under the guidance of George's brother, Basilio. In 1861
the firm helped to develop the Egyptian cotton trade as an alternative to the
American southern states. From 1870 Basilio ran the shipping business.
      The company was British-registered but maintained its contacts in
Greece. The line owned nine steamers on its incorporation in 1897. Basilio's
death in 1897 had the effect of spreading the shares among six family members
which made it difficult to modernise the fleet without capital injection, and in
1901 the firm was sold to Ellerman. It continued to be operated as a separate
entity until 1932. In 1958 Ellerman Papayanni acquired the Mossgiel S.S. Co.
of Glasgow and began containerisation in 1969. Mediterranean services have
continued after the 1973 Ellerman reorganisation and two changes of ownership.
      The majority of the Ellerman Papayanni records are from the years
following the Second World War and none date from the Papayanni family
ownership. There are a number of 1:600 scale models of its ships in the
museum collection.

Records

Finance

Ledgers (agents, voyage, disbursements, clearing, private), 1903-1937,
   1966-1968.

Operational

Particulars of Steamers, 1934.
Particulars of Fleet, 1966.
Trim & Stability Books, 1956, 1968.
Freight Manifests, 1971.
Passenger Record Book, 1949-1972.

Staff

Reference Books, master and mates, 1918-1962.

Miscellaneous

Newscuttings Book, 1964-1970.
B/ELP   1903-1972   11 Boxes 78 Volumes

Reference

Haws, D. *Ellerman Lines*. Hereford, 1989.

Taylor, J. *Ellermans, A Wealth of Shipping*. London, 1976.

Royal Mail Steam Packet Co.

The Royal Mail Steam Packet Company was incorporated by Royal Charter in
1839 to run mail services to the West Indies, Brazil and the River Plate. The
last years of the nineteenth century were a time of stagnation and so it was
purchased relatively cheaply by the brothers John and Owen Philipps in 1903.
In 1910 RMSP acquired PSNC, one of many companies bought as part of a
strategy to set up a major shipping combine. In 1927 Owen Philipps (created
Lord Kylsant in 1923) over-reached himself when he bought White Star. In the
ensuing crash Kylsant was found guilty of publishing a misleading prospectus
and jailed. The group was dismembered and reconstructed. Royal Mail Lines
Ltd. was established in 1932 under the Chairmanship of Lord Essendon, head
of the Furness Withy group and also Chairman of White Star Line. In 1938 it

was able to purchase PSNC and so the two concerns again became linked. In 1965 RMSP became a wholly-owned subsidiary of Furness Withy. It is therefore not surprising that the records of RMSP and PSNC are somewhat intermingled. The main Archives of RMSP is held by the National Maritime Museum but certain items, listed below, are in the PSNC Archives. This museum also holds fine models of *Tagus* (1899) and *Andes* (1939).

Records

Copies of charters, 1839-1921.
Reports on pension and benevolent fund, 1911-1926 with deed, 1904.
Directors' minute books, 1932-1970.
General Meeting minute books, 1932-1964.
Accounts, 1958-1964.
Crew book, 1914-1928.
Rates of pay, 1910.
Historical notes, 1929-1972.
Colon Wharf, Panama, plans and documents, 1885.
Misc. passenger ephemera, 1912-1970
Petitions before Mr. Justice Eve, 1932.
(see also joint committee and other references under PSNC entry).
PSNC   1839-1972   9 Volumes   3 Boxes

Reference

Green, E. and Moss, M. *A Business of National Importance. The Royal Mail Shipping Group, 1902-1937*. London, 1982.

Haws, D. *Royal Mail Line and Nelson Line*. Hereford, 1982.

Shaw Savill and Albion Co.

Shaw Savill and Albion Co. was formed as a limited company in 1882 by the merger of Shaw Savill and Co. of London with Patrick Henderson's Glasgow-based Albion Line. Both ran sail services for cargo and passengers (mainly emigrants) to New Zealand. They joined forces to invest in steamers and to compete with the government-backed New Zealand Shipping Co., also launched in 1882. In the event, both lines shared the mail service and benefited from the development of the refrigerated meat trade. In 1883 Shaw Savill and Albion ordered its first two steamers and negotiated with White Star to use three of its surplus ships. This link continued, with White Star taking a share of ownership. In 1910 Ellerman also took a major share but the line continued to operate separately until White Star was bought by Lord Kylsant in 1926, who then purchased the Ellerman share in 1927. As a result, Shaw Savill and Albion was caught in the Kylsant crash and was acquired by Furness Withy. In association with the British Maritime Trust, it was rebuilt and operated a fleet of cargo liners and a few large passenger liners until the early 1970s. In 1978 a New Zealand and Australian "combi" service to the West Indies was started with Bank Line. From 1980 to 1986 this was an all-container service using one last ship under Shaw Savill and Albion colours.

Records

Sailing cards, c. 1870 in Gracie Beazley collection.
B/GBE
Official guide and handbook, 1910.
Sailing bills, timetables, 1880, 1911, 1938 1901.
Passenger list and logbooks, 1887, 1915, 1926 and 1936.
Miscellaneous Voyage ephemera, 1892-1901.
SAS   1880-1936   approx. 2 Boxes

References

Middlemiss, N.L. *Furness-Houlder Lines*. Newcastle, 1991.

Waters, S.D. *Shaw Savill Line, One Hundred Years of Trading*. Christchurch, 1961.

Straits Steamship Company

In 1866 George and Walter Mansfield, Singapore ship chandlers, obtained the agency for Holts Blue Funnel Line (Ocean Steam Ship Co.) and became one of the great Asian trading companies. In 1903 Mansfield became a limited liability company with Alfred Holt and Co. as principal shareholders. Mansfield became an agent for Imperial Airways in 1933, then for other airlines, survived World War II and merged with the Straits Steamship Company. A Dutchman, T.C. Bogaardt, established a network of feeders for Blue Funnel between 1872 and 1890, when he set up the Straits Steamship Company, a joint venture between Alfred Holt and Kim Seng and Co. when an Anglo-Chinese joint venture was a novelty. In 1914 Holts took it over with Mansfield and Co. as general managers. The firm served outlying ports and by 1932 had fifty-five ships from small coasters to large passenger ships. It suffered badly due to the Japanese invasion and by 1957 diversified into operating Malayan Airways, engineering, transportation, insurance, property development and data processing.

Records

Board minutes, 1946-1947.
W. Mansfield and Co. Ltd., minutes and balance sheets, 1903-1923.
Directors' reports and accounts, 1914-1923.
Balance sheets, 1947-1951 (including Malayan Airways).
Malaysian Airways annual reports, c. 1950-c. 1960.
Directors' paper (including Siam Steam Navigation Co. Ltd.).
Working accounts of various steamers, 1913-1917.
Correspondence re: purchase of shares by Ocean Steamship Co., 1914-1919.
Journal, 1903-1922.
Management papers, Sir S. McTier and W.H. McNeill, 1932-1962.
Reports on policy, 1950-1956.
Singapore evacuation reports, 1942.
Mansfield and Co. letters, 1868-1931, 1945-1949.
Malayan Airways negotiations, 1932-1949.
Shore personnel staff movements, 1942-1945.
Coal contract, Admiralty supply at Singapore, 1896.
Pilgrim ordinance and rules, 1929.
Notebook re: Mansfield and Co., Singapore agency, 1900-1918.
Ship details, 1934-1939.
World War II incidents.
Press cuttings, brochures, etc., re: new developments, 1976-1982.
Menu cards, c. 1950-1960.
Photographs of docks, ships, etc., c. 1860-1977.
OA   1868-1977   (See Ocean Steam Ship Co. Ltd.)

Reference

Falkus, M. *The Blue Funnel Legend. A History of the Ocean Steam Ship Company, 1865-1973*. London, 1990.

White Star Line

Thomas Ismay, sailing shipowner and a director of the National Line, bought the name and goodwill of the defunct White Star Line of Australian sailing packets in 1867. In 1868-1869, with the assistance of Gustav Schwabe, a Liverpool financier, he set up the Oceanic Steam Navigation Co. Ltd., which was always known as the White Star Line. Four large ships were ordered from Schwabe's nephew's shipyard, Harland and Wolff of Belfast. They were large, fast, with better accommodation, higher pressure boilers (and so more economical) than their competitors. Sailings started in 1870 and were an immediate success. In 1873 the wreck of the *Atlantic* with heavy loss of life only slowed temporarily its rise in the intensely competitive transatlantic trade. It strengthened its position by a traffic-sharing agreement with the Inman Line and a share of the mail contract in 1876. Ismay, Imrie and Co., the managers, also ran a fleet of large iron and steel sailing ships until 1895. In 1881 a trans-Pacific service was started from San Francisco to Hong Kong, followed by a UK-New Zealand service with Shaw, Savill and Albion. In 1888-1889 it began to buy cargo and cattle steamers as well as large luxurious passenger liners of moderate speed, a policy which ultimately led to the 45,000-ton sisters *Olympic*, *Titanic* and *Britannic* via the 17,500-ton *Oceanic* (1899). Thomas Ismay died in 1899 and in 1902 his creation was sold to the International Mercantile Marine. Its British management and registry was retained; services with other British lines in the IMM, such as Dominion, were rationalised and the "main line" service was moved in 1907 from Liverpool to Southampton from where the ill-fated *Titanic* left on its maiden voyage in April 1912. The fleet, with its big passenger ships, made a major contribution to the 1914-1918 war effort and carried in total about one million soldiers and four million tons of cargo. It also lost major ships, such as the *Britannic*, sunk in the Dardanelles in 1915, but was able to obtain two ex-German liners as reparations. In 1926 it was purchased by Lord Kylsant, whose subsequent crash caused the cancellation of an order for a new 60,000-ton liner and the merger with Cunard in 1934. The motor ships *Britannic* (1930) and *Georgic* (1932) were retained on the Liverpool-New York service.

It is likely that the line's Archives were destroyed some time after the merger with Cunard. Little survives in the main Cunard Archives at Liverpool University while the museum's Cunard holdings contain quite a good selection of plans of ships built after 1900 and the MDHB collection for pre-1900 vessels. The bulk of the museum's holdings are in the Bryson collection, together with documents deposited by Ayrton, Alderson Smith, solicitors, on behalf of the Ismay family. There is also material specific to *Titanic* listed in volume 2, Special Collections. The museum has original builder's models of *Oceanic* (1871), *Garfield* (1882, Ismay Imrie), *Teutonic* (1889), *California* (1890, Ismay Imrie), *Oceanic* (1899), *Cretic* (1902), *Cedric* (1903), *Titanic* (1911), *Homeric* (1922, ex-*Columbus*), and also the bell and whistle from *Britannic* (1932).

Records

Bryson Collection

Monthly office accounts of J.B. Ismay, 1908-1912.
Correspondence, C. McIver, W.S. Graves, T.H. Ismay re: advance for Beaver
        Line, also F.M. Radcliffe (partner in Ayrton, Alderson Smith),
        1894-1911.

Letters re: disposal of papers of T.H. Ismay involving members of the family, 1910-1914, including guarantee of destruction by waste paper merchants and lists of papers to be destroyed.

Correspondence, Mrs. T.H. Ismay and Norman Shaw, architect, re: memorial to T.H. Ismay, 1899-1900, also with designers and craftsmen.

Provisional agreement with J.P. Morgan and Co. re: acquisition of White Star and four other liners, 1902, with correspondence and notice of Ordinary General Meeting, 1902.

Papers re: jewellery, pictures, etc., of Mrs. J.F. Ismay, 1957-1963.

File re: estate of T.H. Ismay, 1907-1935.

Bills re: White Star offices, 1922-1923.

Family settlement papers, 1863-1956.

Company pension fund papers, 1938.

Papers re: estate of Ismay family in Northamptonshire, twentieth century.

D/B/174   1863-1963   3 Boxes

Ayrton, Alderson Smith section

Correspondence with P.A.S Franklin, New York, re: resignation of J. Bruce Ismay from the board of IMM, 1916.

Correspondence, J. Bruce Ismay to Lord Mayor of Liverpool re: extension of Liverpool Seamen's Pension Fund (founded by T.H. Ismay) to provide pensions for seamen's widows, 1912.

Letter from Chief Engineer of *Olympic* re: maiden voyage, 1911, with other letters including one on the coal situation affecting speed of *Olympic* and *Titanic*

Papers re: Ismay coat of arms and window in Liverpool Cathedral, 1913.

Papers re: Sandheys, Mossley Hill, house of J. Bruce Ismay, 1909-1914, with personal papers, 1912-1917.

Correspondence, P.A.S. Franklin, J. Bruce Ismay, Captain E.J. Smith of *Olympic*, etc., re: *Olympic* to show that J. Bruce Ismay was opposed to fast running of steamers, 1911.

Typescript notes on Church of Thurstaston, where T.H. Ismay lived (Ismay was a benefactor), 1893.

DX/504   1893-1917   1 Box

Photo Albums, *Teutonic* (1897) and *Oceanic* (1899)   4 Volumes

Cunard plans collection.   103 Bundles

MDHB plans collection.   1 Folio

References

Anderson, R. *White Star*. Prescot, 1964.

Oldham, W.J. *The Ismay Line*. Liverpool, 1961.

Yeoward Line

Yeoward Brothers established a fruit importing business from the Canaries, Spain and Portugal to Liverpool in 1894, using chartered tonnage. In 1900 it bought its first second-hand ship. In 1903 it started building new ships with passenger accommodation which proved popular. After the sale of two ships in 1939 and the loss of another three in the Second World War, Yeoward was left with *Alca*, which was scrapped in 1955. It then reverted to chartering until the Aznar Line of Bilbao took over its services. The company continues in the fruit trade, with interests in travel, road haulage and distribution.

Records

Aquila passengers' list, 1920.
DX/1030
Holiday cruises publicity material, 1933.
DX/915
Voyage ephemera from *Alca*, 1951.
DX/1016

Reference

Barry, T.W.S. *Sunward by Yeoward. The Story of Yeoward of Liverpool – The First 100 Years*. Cambridge, 1994.

Zillah Shipping Co. Ltd.

Founded in 1895 by William Savage of Warrington, the Zillah Shipping and Carrying Co. Ltd. started with the wooden steamer, *Zillah*, both the company and ship being named after his wife. In 1906 the company moved to Liverpool with eight steamers in the coal trade to Ireland and the North Wales stone trade. From 1914 to 1948 the company ordered all its new ships from the Lytham Shipbuilding and Engineering Co. and most of these records relate to these. Coast Lines bought the company in 1948 and it was finally phased out in 1967. The museum holds eleven ship models of the company, 1896-1913.

Records

Cargo books (9), 1950-1955.
Company regulations, 1956.
Diary (unused), 1959.
Ship photographs, c. 1950.
Specifications and capacity plans, 1908, 1920-1930.
Anchor and chain test certificates, 1915-1947.
Classification, boiler and engine certificates, 1920-1941.
Miscellaneous papers re: ships' cargo and lifesaving appliances, 1940-1943.
SAS/29/23/1-10   1 Box

Plans, general arrangements
SAS/DC

Reference

Waine, C.V. *Steam Coasters and Short Sea Traders*. Wolverhampton, 1976.